JOKES FOR EVERY DAY

Laughs Guaranteed

■ SCHOLASTIC

For Samuel, my most favourite penguin,
love Uncle Toby

This edition first published in the UK by Scholastic, 2024
1 London Bridge, London, SE1 9BG
Scholastic Ireland, 89E Lagan Road, Dublin Industrial Estate,
Glasnevin, Dublin, D11 HP5

SCHOLASTIC and associated logos are trademarks, and/or
registered trademarks of Scholastic Inc.

Text by Toby Reynolds © Scholastic, 2014 - 2024
Cover by Aaron Blecha © Scholastic, 2024
Inside illustrations by Andrew Pinder © Scholastic, 2014 - 2024

This material previously appeared in:
Gigglers: School Jokes
Gigglers: Disgusting Jokes
Gigglers: Sporty Jokes
Gigglers: Animal Jokes

ISBN 978 0702 34062 8

A CIP catalogue record for this book is available from the British Library.
All rights reserved.

This book is sold subject to the condition that it shall not, by way of trade or
otherwise, be lent, hired out or otherwise circulated in any form of binding
or cover other than that in which it is published. No part of this publication
may be reproduced, stored in a retrieval system, or transmitted in any form,
or by any other means (electronic, mechanical, photocopying, recording or
otherwise) without prior written permission of Scholastic Limited.

Printed and bound in Great Britain by Clays Ltd, Elcograf S.p.A
Paper made from wood grown in sustainable forests and other controlled sources.

MIX
Paper | Supporting
responsible forestry
FSC® C018072

1 3 5 7 9 10 8 6 4 2

www.scholastic.co.uk

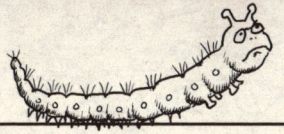

Contents

ANIMAL JOKES 7
Funny Farms 9
Jungle Gags 22
Potty Pets 26
Silly Sea Life 36
Bonkers Birds 43
Comedy Creepy Crawlies 50
Slapstick Savannah 59
Arctic Antics 65
Ridiculous Reptiles 69
Amusing Amphibians 77
Wacky Woodland 80
Mind-blowing Mash-ups 88

SPORTY JOKES	**97**
Absurd Athletics	98
Archery Antics	106
Badminton Buffoonery	109
Barmy Basketball	111
Boisterous Boxing	116
Bonkers Bowling	120
Brilliant Baseball	122
Comical Cricket	124
Cycling Capers	127
Funny Football	131
Goofy Golf	142
Gymnastics Gags	146
Hilarious Horse Racing	148
Hysterical Hockey	155
Incredible Ice Skating	157

Martial Arts Mayhem	158
Ridiculous Rugby	160
Side-Splitting Swimming	162
Silly Sailing	166
Spectacular Sports Day	169
Tennis Tomfoolery	173
Terrific Trampolining	176
Wacky Weightlifting	178
Witty Wrestling	179
Smashing Sports Books	180
SCHOOL JOKES	**183**
Ready for School	184
Our Quirky Head Teacher	188
Tee-hee-hee Teachers	194
English Class Capers	200
Side-Splitting Science Lab	208
Rowdy Music Lesson	215

School Lunchtimes LOLs	**222**
Hilarious History Class	**229**
Mayhem Maths Class	**237**
Silly Sports Class	**246**
Goofy Geography	**254**
Art Class Antics	**261**
Laughable Library	**266**
Hopeless Homework	**271**
DISGUSTING JOKES	**277**
Toilet Tomfoolery	**278**
Windy Wisecracks	**287**

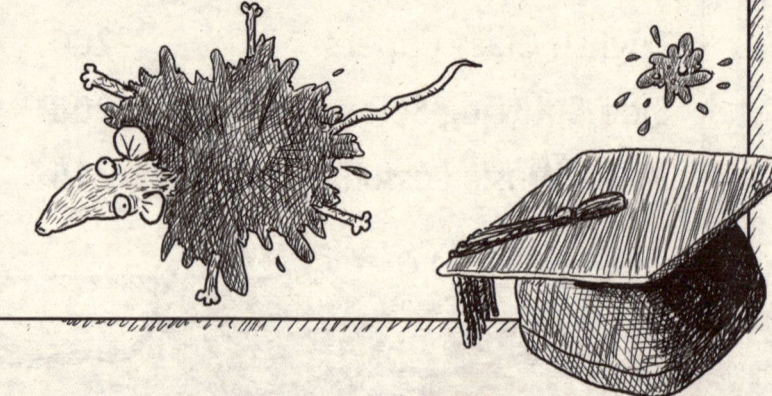

Funny Farms

Q. What did the horse say when he finished his meal?
A. "That's the last straw!"

Q. What is the difference between a horse and a duck?
A. One goes quick and the other goes quack!

Q. What did the horse say when it fell over?
A. "I've fallen and I can't giddy up!"

Q. Why did the horse eat with its mouth open?
A. Because it had bad stable manners.

Q. Why did the pony have to gargle?
A. Because it was a little horse!

Q. What do you call a horse that lives at the farm next door?
A. A neigh-bour!

Q. Why did the thrill-seeking farmer stand behind the horse?
A. He was hoping to get a kick out of it.

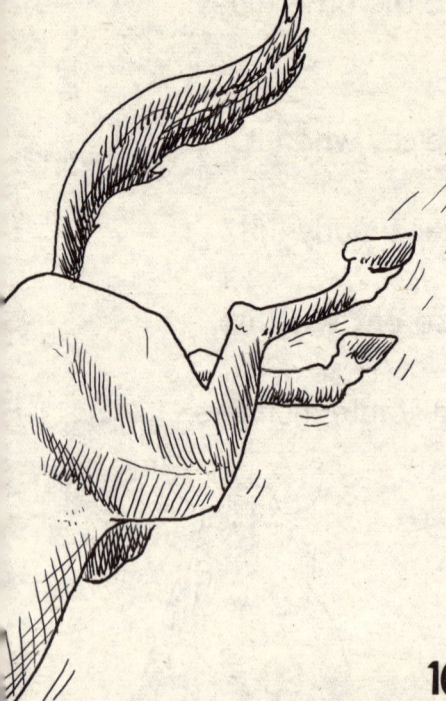

Q. What kind of farm animal goes OOM?
A. A cow walking backwards!

Q. Why did the farmer tell the geese to be quiet?
A. He was tired of their fowl language.

Q. What's a cow's favourite city?
A. Moo York!

Q. What is the difference between a chicken and an elephant?
A. An elephant can get chicken pox, but a chicken can't get elephant pox.

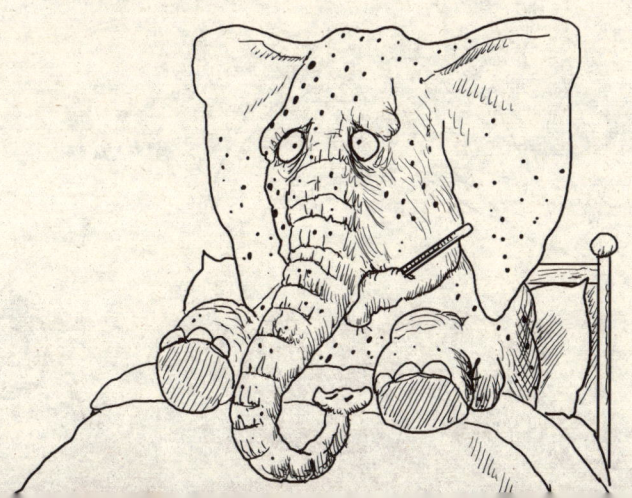

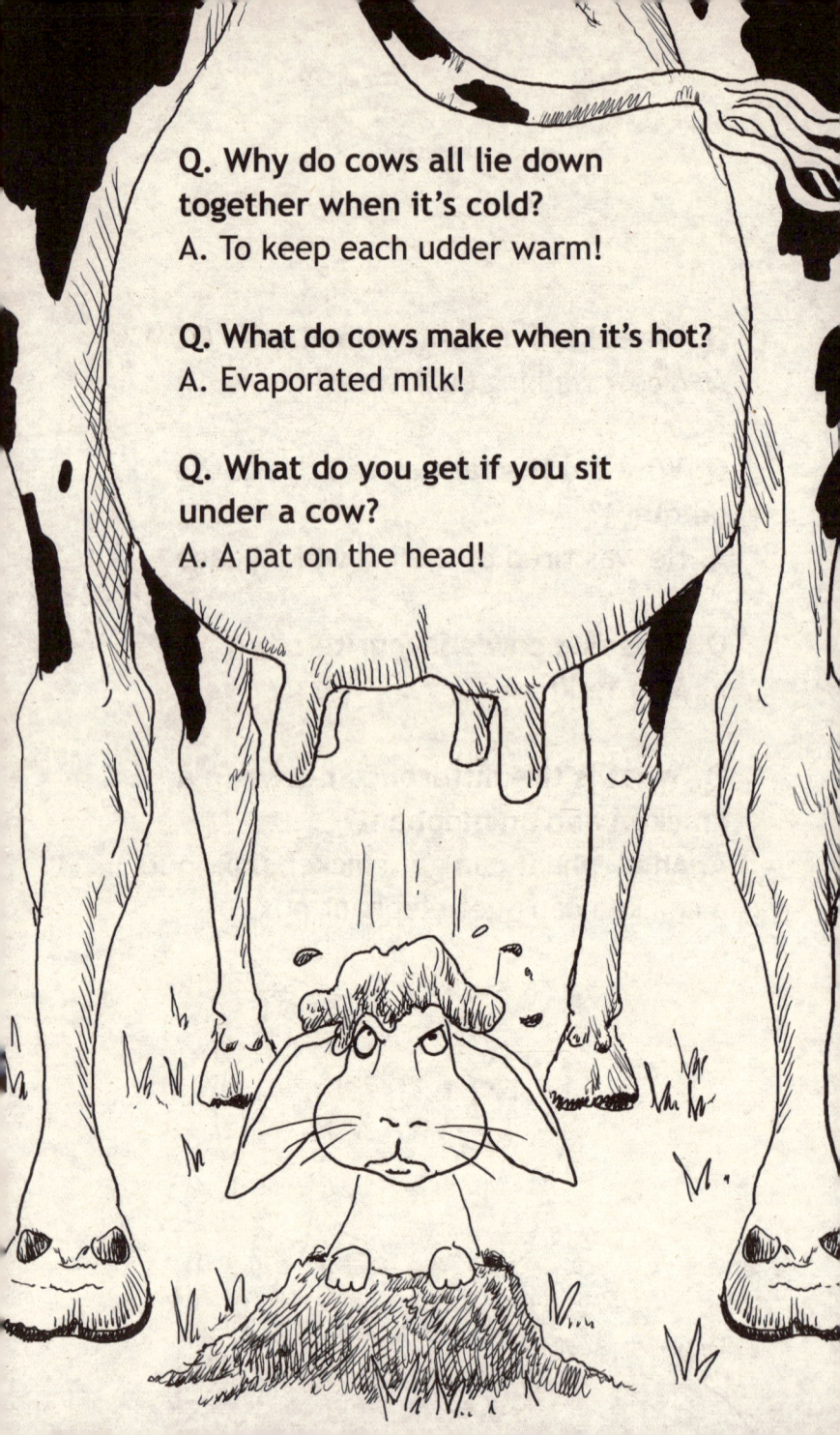

Q. Why do cows all lie down together when it's cold?
A. To keep each udder warm!

Q. What do cows make when it's hot?
A. Evaporated milk!

Q. What do you get if you sit under a cow?
A. A pat on the head!

Q. What happened to the cow that ran away from the farm?
A. He was never herd of again!

Q. What did the mummy cow say to the baby cow?
A. It's pasture bedtime.

Knock, knock.
Who's there?
Cows go.
Cows go who?
Cows go moo, not who!

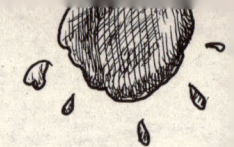

Q. How do farmers count their cows?
A. They use a cow-culator.

Q. Why do cows love joke books?
A. Because they love to be amoosed!

Q. Why is it hard to have a conversation with a goat?
A. Because they keep butting in!

Q. What does a cow read every morning?
A. A moos-paper.

Q. What do you call a goat dressed like a clown?
A. A silly billy.

Q. When did the goat realize he was a goat?
A. When he was just a little kid.

Q. What do you call a thief that steals pigs?
A. A ham burglar!

Q. What is a pig's favourite ballet?
A. Swine Lake!

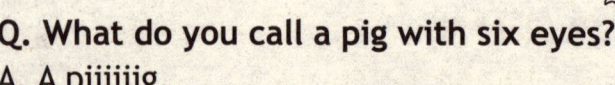

Q. What do you call a pig with six eyes?
A. A piiiiiig.

Knock, Knock.
Who's there?
Oink, oink.
Oink, oink who?
Make up your mind – are you a pig or an owl?

Q. What is the fastest way to take a pig to hospital?
A. By ham-bulance!

Q. Is it true that pigs take two baths a day?
A. No, that story is just a load of hogwash.

Q. Why is a pig the best actor on the farm?
A. He loves to ham it up and hog all the attention.

Q. How did the farmer fit more pigs on his farm?
A. He built a sty-scraper!

Q. What is a pig's favourite Shakespeare play?
A. Hamlet.

Q. How do pig's explain the beginnings of the universe?
A. With the Pig Bang Theory.

Q. Why was the pig sacked from his job as a TV talk show host?
A. He turned out to be a big boar.

Q. What farm vehicles do pigs love to drive?
A. Pig-up trucks!

Q. What animal sounds like a sheep but isn't?
A. A baa-boon!

Q. How does the farmer greet the pigs at Christmas?
A. Merry Christmas to ewe!

Q. How many sheep does it take to knit a jumper?
A. Don't be silly – sheep can't knit!

Q. What do you call a sheep with no legs?
A. A cloud.

Q. Where do sheep get their wool cut?
A. At the baa-baa shop!

Q. Why was the sheep arrested on the motorway?
A. Because she did a ewe-turn!

Q. Where does a sheep wash?
A. In the baa-th tub!

Q. Where do sheep go on holiday?
A. To the baa-hamas.

Q. What did the ambitious sheep want to do?
A. Wool the world.

Q. What kind of car does a sheep dream of driving?
A. A Lamb-borghini.

Q. What was the sheep's favourite swimming style?
A. The baa-ckstroke!

Jungle Gags

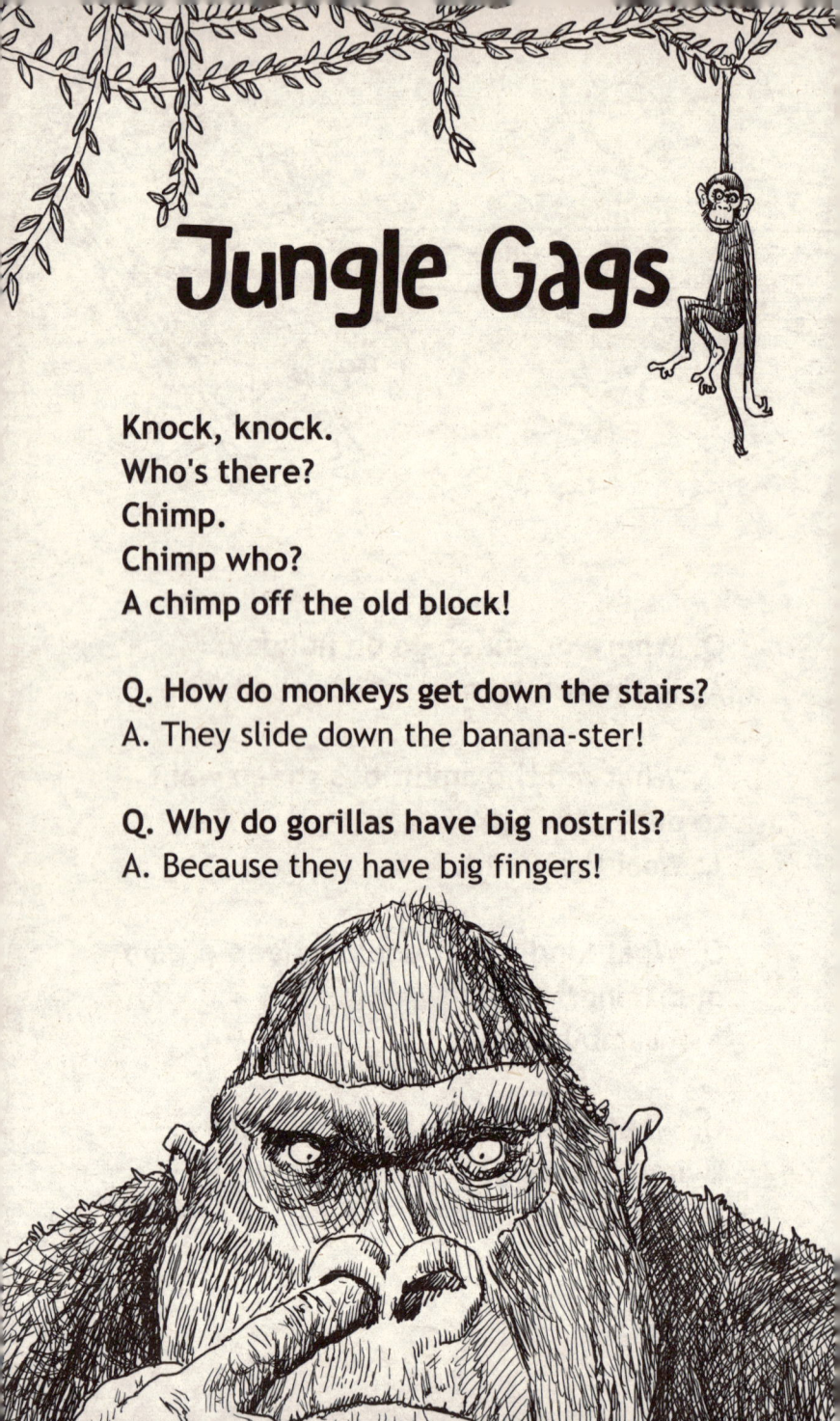

Knock, knock.
Who's there?
Chimp.
Chimp who?
A chimp off the old block!

Q. How do monkeys get down the stairs?
A. They slide down the banana-ster!

Q. Why do gorillas have big nostrils?
A. Because they have big fingers!

Q. What do you call a monkey with a banana in each ear?
A. Anything you want, it can't hear you.

Knock, knock.
Who's there?
Gorilla.
Gorilla who?
Gorilla-d cheese for me, please!

Q. What kind of key opens a banana?
A. A monkey!

Q. Why did the monkey like the banana?
A. Because it had appeal!

Q. What do you call a monkey who's training to be a wizard?
A. Hairy Potter.

Q. Where do chimps get their gossip?
A. On the ape vine!

Q. How do you keep a monkey in suspense?
A. I'll tell you tomorrow.

Q. Why did the tiger lose at poker?
A. Because he was playing against a cheetah!

Q. What is the fiercest flower in the jungle?
A. A tiger lily!

Q. How is a tiger like an army sergeant?
A. They both wear stripes with pride.

Q. Who went into the tiger's den and came out alive?
A. The tiger!

Q. On which day of the week do tigers eat people?
A. Chews-day!

Q. What's the silliest name you can give a tiger?
A. Spot!

Potty Pets

Q. How did the cat feel after eating a duck?
A. A little down in the mouth!

Q. What is a cat's favourite TV programme?
A. The Mews at Ten!

Q. What did the cat do when he saw a mouse?
A. Made a feline for it!

Q. When is it bad luck to see a black cat?
A. When you're a mouse!

Q. What does a cat with stinky breath need?
A. Mouse wash!

Q. What happened to the cat that swallowed a ball of wool?
A. She had mittens!

Q. What do you call a cat that has just eaten a duck?
A. A duck-filled fatty puss!

Q. What has twelve legs, three tails and can't see?
A. Three blind mice!

Q. What is the biggest mouse in the world?
A. A Hippopota-mouse!

Q. What do you give to a drowning mouse?
A. Mouse-to-mouse resuscitation!

Q. Why was the mouse afraid of the river?
A. Because of all the catfish.

Q. What is small, furry and brilliant at sword fighting?
A. A mouse-keteer!

Q. What goes dot, dot, dash, squeak?
A. Mouse code!

Q. How do mice celebrate when they move to a new home?
A. They throw a mouse-warming party!

Q. What kind of dog does Dracula have?
A. A bloodhound!

Q. What do you call a dog magician?
A. A Labracadabrador.

Q. What do you call a dog on a stick?
A. A lolli-pup.

Q. Why do dogs bury bones in the ground?
A. Because you can't bury them in trees!

Q. What happened to the dog that swallowed a torch?
A. It barked with de-light!

Q. Which American city do dogs like best?
A. New Yorkie.

Q. What did the cat say to the dog?
A. Check meow-t!

Q. Where did the dog keep his car?
A. In the car bark.

Q. What kind of dog likes taking baths?
A. A shampoodle!

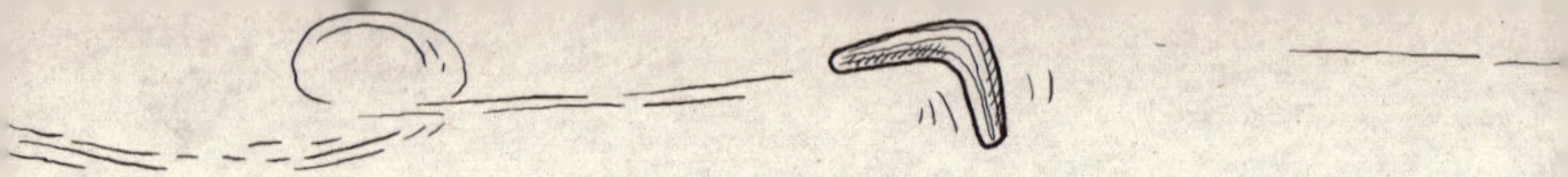

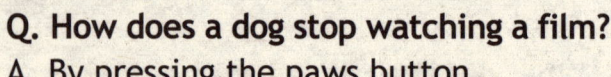

Q. How does a dog stop watching a film?
A. By pressing the paws button.

Q. What do Dalmatians say after a satisfying meal?
A. That really hit the spots!

Knock, knock.
Who's there?
Rabbit.
Rabbit who?
Rabbit up neatly – it's fragile!

Q. Why do Australian dogs cross the road twice?
A. Because they are always trying to fetch boomerangs!

Q. Why did the bald man put a rabbit on his head?
A. Because he wanted a head of hare!

Q. How do rabbits travel?
A. By hare-oplane.

Q. What did the rabbit give his girlfriend when he asked her to marry him?
A. A 14 carrot ring!

Q. Where do rabbits go after their wedding?
A. On their bunnymoon!

Q. What do you call a sunburnt rabbit?
A. A hot cross bunny.

Q. How do you know that eating carrots is good for your eyes?
A. Because you never see rabbits wearing glasses!

Q. How can you tell which rabbits are getting old?
A. Look for the grey hares.

Q. What's the difference between a healthy rabbit and an odd rabbit?
A. One is a fit bunny and the other is a bit funny!

Q. Why did the rabbit build herself a new house?
A. She was fed up with the hole thing!

Silly Sea Life

Q. Why are fish so well educated?
A. They are always in schools!

Q. What do you call a fish with no eyes?
A. A fsh!

**Knock, knock.
Who's there?
Tuna.
Tuna who?
Tuna your banjo and you can join our band!**

Q. Which fish go to heaven when they die?
A. Angelfish.

Q. Who's the most frightening fish in the ocean?
A. Jack the kipper.

Q. Why do fish boots keep your ankles warm?
A. Because they have electric 'eels.

Q. What did the fish do when his piano sounded odd?
A. He called the piano tuna.

Q. Why did the shark cross the Great Barrier Reef?
A. To get to the other tide.

Q. What type of burgers do sharks love?
A. Quarter flounders with cheese.

Q. Why won't sharks eat clownfish?
A. They taste funny!

Q. What is a shark's favourite type of sandwich?
A. Peanut butter and jellyfish!

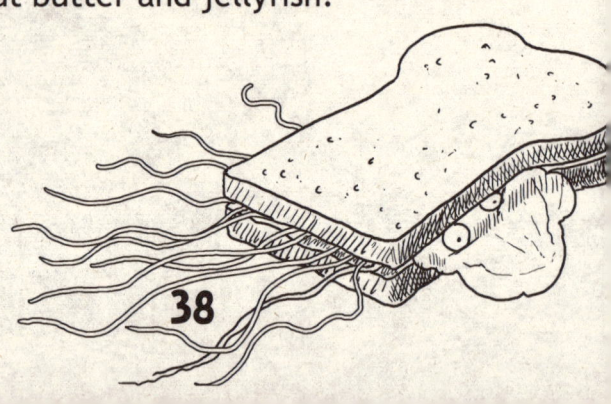

Q. Who delivers presents to sharks at Christmas?
A. Santa Jaws!

Q. What do you call the mushy stuff stuck between a great white shark's teeth?
A. Slow swimmers!

Q. Which sharks work on a building site?
A. Hammerhead sharks.

Q. How do you make a shark laugh?
A. Tell a whale of a tale.

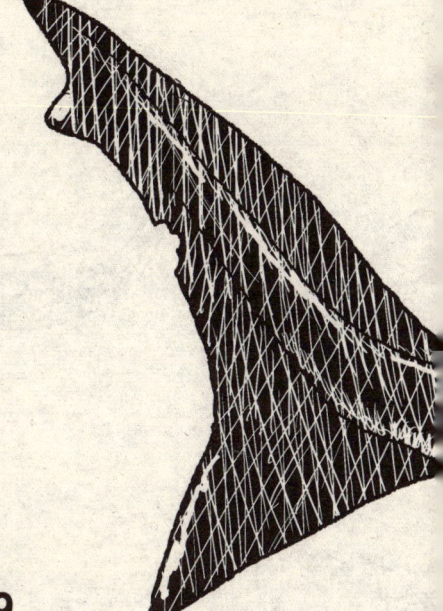

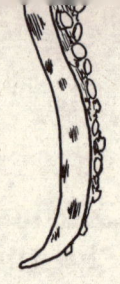

Q. What hobby does a shark like best?
A. Anything he can sink his teeth into.

Q. What did the shark say to the whale?
A. What are you blubbering on about?

Q. What did the dolphin say when he bumped into the whale?
A. I didn't do it on porpoise!

Q. Why did the fish want to be an astronaut?
A. He wanted to explore trout-er space!

Q. How do you make an octopus laugh?
A. With ten-tickles

Q. Did you hear about the two eels that had a race?
A. It ended in a tie!

Q. Who held the baby octopus to ransom?
A. Squidnappers!

Q. Why are goldfish orange?
A. The water makes them rusty!

Q. What did the magician say to the fisherman?
A. Pick a cod, any cod!

Bonkers Birds

Q. Why do two sparrows in a nest never argue?
A. Because they don't want to fall out.

Q. What do sparrow families do on Saturday afternoon?
A. They go on peck-nics!

Q. What do you call a very rude pigeon?
A. A mockingbird!

Q. What time does a duck wake up?
A. At the quack of dawn!

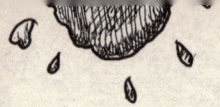

Q. Who stole the soap?
A. The robber ducky!

Q. What was the goal of the detective duck?
A. To quack the case

Knock, knock.
Who's there?
Quacker!
Quacker who?
Quacker another bad joke and I'm leaving!

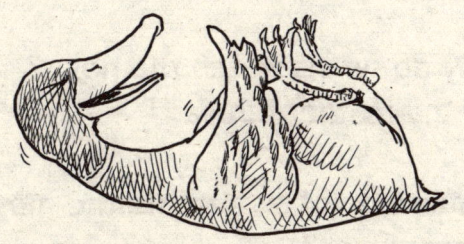

Q. What did the duck do after he read all these jokes?
A. He quacked up!

Q. What says "Quick, Quick!"?
A. A duck with the hiccups.

Q. What does a duck do first when making an omelette?
A. He quacks some eggs.

Q. What do ducks watch on TV?
A. Duck-umentaries!

Q. Why do swans watch the news?
A. For the feather forecast!

Q. Which side of a swan has the most feathers?
A. The outside!

Q. Why did the goose fly south for the winter?
A. Because it was too far to walk.

Q. What do you say at the reception of the fowl hotel?
A. I would like to chicken to my room please!

Q. What bird is helpful at dinner?
A. A swallow!

Q. What do you call a poorly eagle?
A. Illegal!

Q. What's the difference between bird flu and swine flu?
A. If you have bird flu, you need tweet-ment but if you have swine flu, you need oink-ment.

Q. Which bird can never catch its breath?
A. A puffin!

Q. How do you catch a unique puffin?
A. Unique up on it.

Q. How many birds does it take to change a light bulb?
A. Toucan do it.

Q. Why do hummingbirds hum?
A. Because they've forgotten the words!

Q. Why do seagulls live by the sea?
A. Because if they lived by the bay they would be bagels.

Comedy Creepy Crawlies

Q. What do insects learn at school?
A. Moth-matics!

Q. What insect lives on nothing?
A. A moth, because it eats holes.

Q. What's the biggest moth in the world?
A. A mam-moth!

Q. What does a caterpillar do on New Year's Day?
A. It turns over a new leaf!

Q. What is the definition of a caterpillar?
A. A worm in a fur coat!

Q. What has fifty legs but can't walk?
A. Half a centipede!

Q. What was the snail doing on the motorway?
A. About a mile a day.

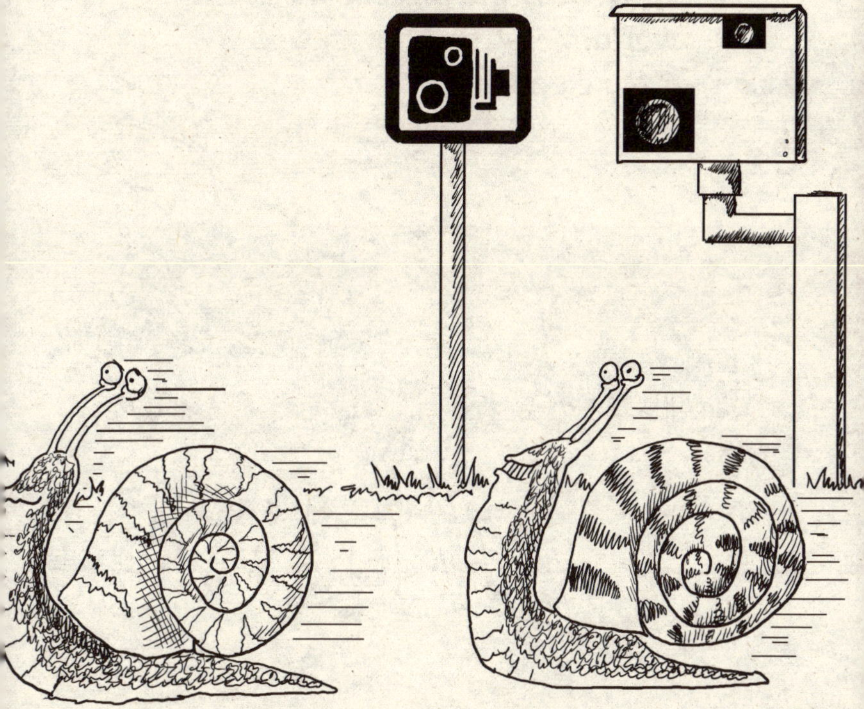

Knock, Knock.
Who's there?
Wood ant!
Wood ant who?
Don't be afraid. Wood ant harm a fly!

Q. Why was the baby ant confused?
A. Because all of his uncles were ants!

Q. What is the biggest ant in the world?
A. An eleph-ant!

Q. What kind of ant is good at maths?
A. An account-ant.

Q. What do you call 100-year-old ants?
A. Antiques.

Q. What do you call an ant that likes to be alone?
A. Independ-ant.

Q. What do you call an ant that skips school?
A. A tru-ant.

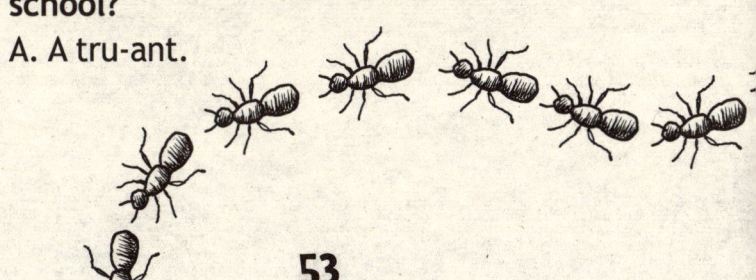

Q. What did the spider say to the fly on Halloween?
A. The web is the trick and you are the treat!

Q. Why don't anteaters get sick?
A. Because they are full of antibodies!

Q. What do you call an ant with frog legs?
A. An ant-phibian!

Q. What are spider webs good for?
A. Spiders!

Q. How do spiders communicate?
A. Through the World Wide Web.

Q. What kinds of doctors are like spiders?
A. Spin doctors!

Q. What does a spider do when he gets angry?
A. He goes up the wall!

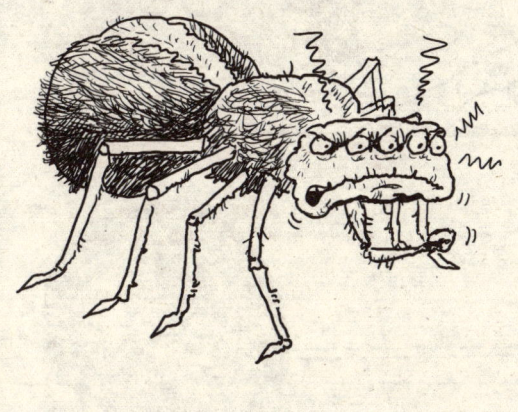

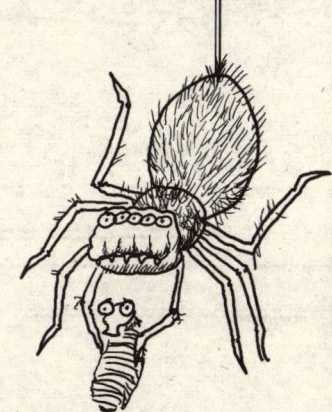

Q. What did the spider say when he broke his new web?
A. Darn it!

Q. Why did the spider get a job in IT?
A. She was a great web designer!

Q. Why did the spider buy a sports car?
A. So he could take it out for a spin!

Q. What do spiders eat in Paris?
A. French flies!

Q. What do you call two recently married spiders?
A. Newly webs!

Q. Why do spiders have eight legs?
A. Because if they had six they would be insects!

Q. Why do spiders spin webs?
A. Because they can't knit!

Q. What is a spider's favourite day?
A. Fly-day!

Q. What is a spider's favourite sport?
A. Fly fishing!

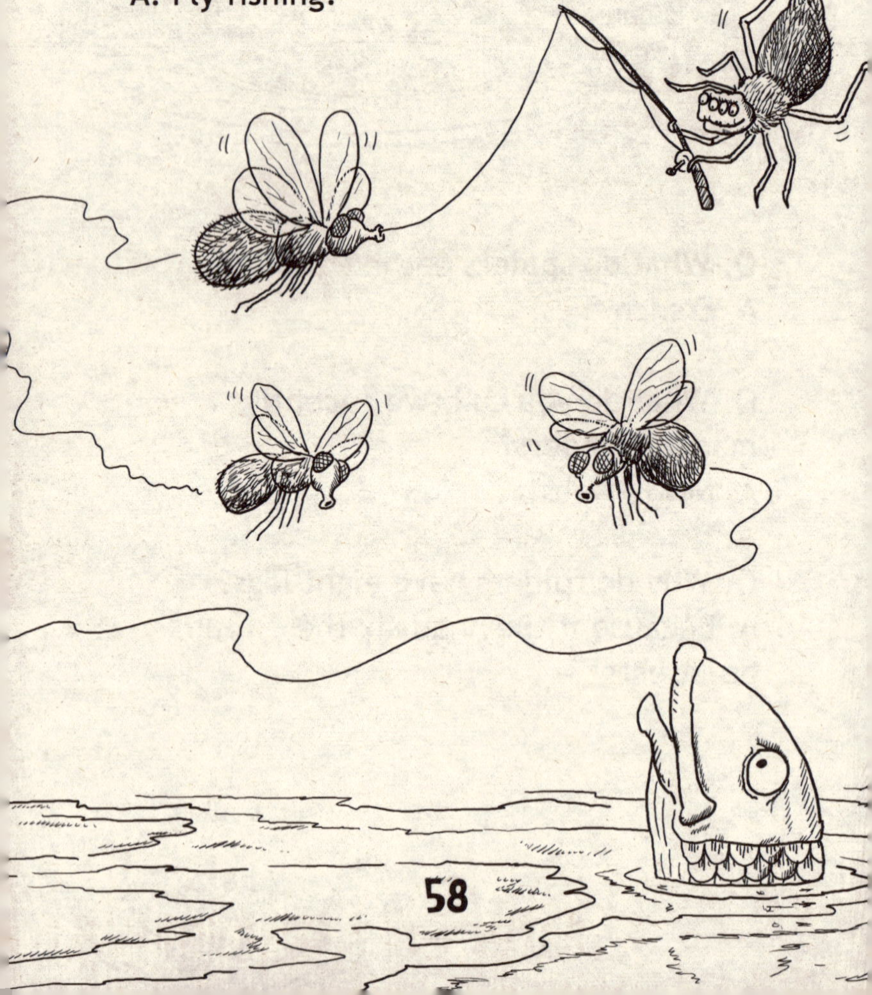

Slapstick Savannah

Q. Why do cheetahs always eat raw meat?
A. Because they don't know how to cook.

Q. Why are elephants such bad dancers?
A. Because they have two left feet!

Q. What's big and grey and protects you from the rain?
A. An umbrella-phant!

Q. Why did the leopard hide in the tall grass?
A. He didn't want to be spotted.

Q. What's the difference between African elephants and Indian Elephants?
A. About 3,000 miles.

Q. What's as big as an elephant, but weighs nothing?
A. An elephant's shadow.

Q. What do you call an elephant that never takes a bath?
A. A smelly-phant!

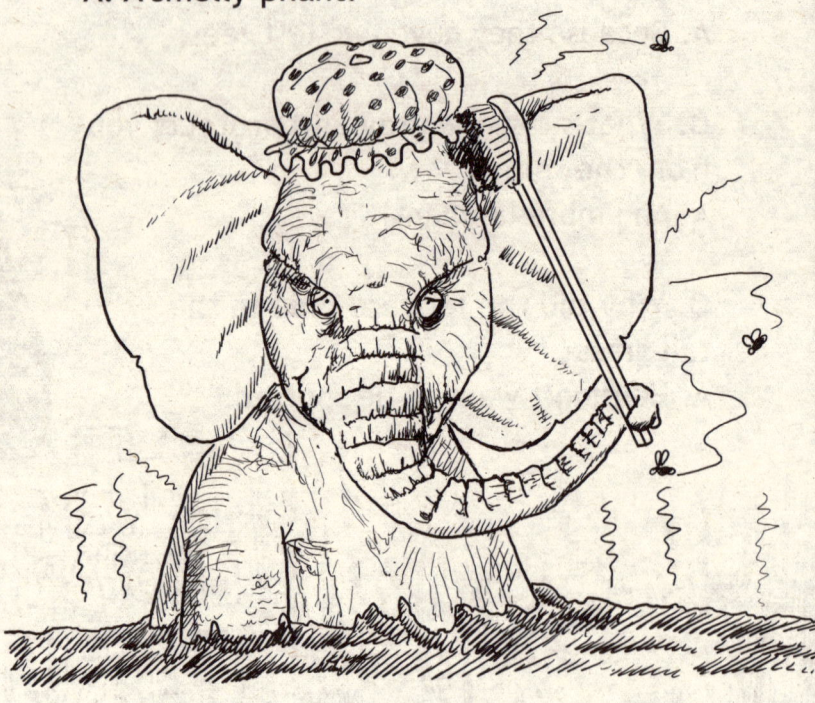

Q. Why did the elephant cross the road?
A. Because it was the chicken's day off!

Q. What's big and grey and flies upwards?
A. An ele-copter!

Q. What do you call an elephant that didn't understand any of these jokes?
A. Dumbo!

Q. What's green and hangs from trees?
A. Giraffe snot!

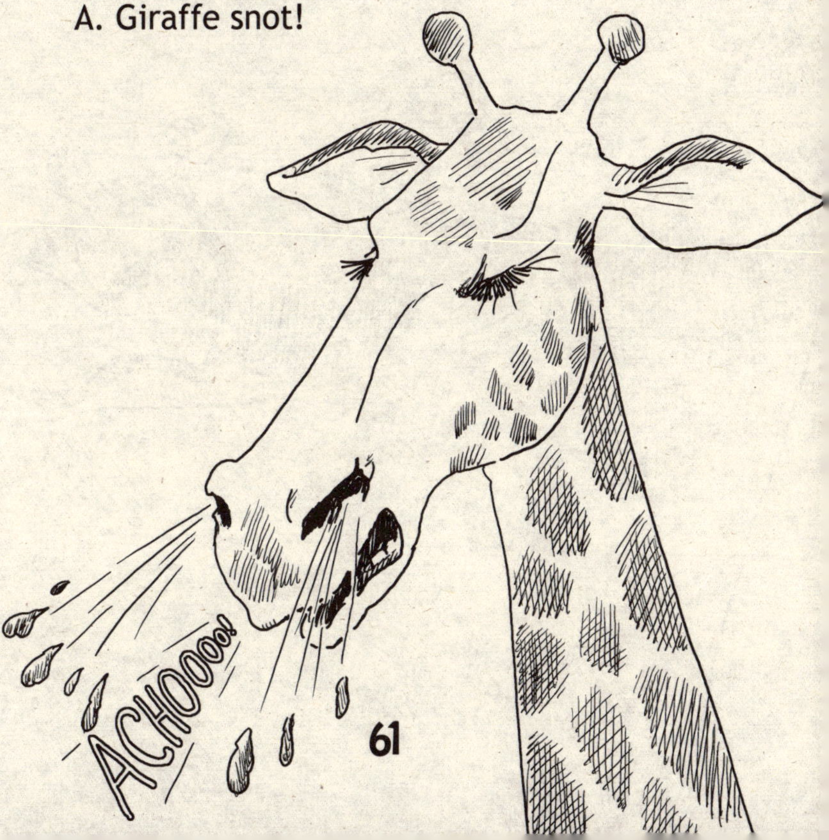

Q. Why are giraffes slow to apologize?
A. It takes them a while to swallow their pride.

Q. Why was the giraffe late?
A. Because he got caught in a giraffic jam!

Q. Why don't giraffes like to go to the playground?
A. Because the monkeys use them as slides.

Q. What's the difference between an injured lion and a wet day?
A. One pours with rain, the other roars with pain!

**Knock, knock.
Who's there?
Omar.
Omar who?
Omar goodness, there's a huge lion behind you!**

Q. What does a lion say to his pride before they go hunting?
A. Let us prey.

Q. How does a lion sail a boat?
A. He uses r-oars.

Q. What do you call a lion wearing a flowery dress?
A. A dandelion.

Q. What is a lion's favourite food?
A. Baked beings!

Q. Why was the lion-tamer fined?
A. He parked on a yellow lion!

Arctic Antics

Q. What kind of fish do penguins catch at night?
A. Starfish.

Q. What did one emperor penguin say to the other?
A. Nothing, they just gave each other the cold shoulder.

Q. Why do penguins carry so many fish in their beaks?
A. Because they haven't got any pockets.

Q. Why did the penguin cross the ice?
A. To go with the floe!

Q. What do penguins put in salads?
A. Iceberg lettuce!

Q. What do penguins wear on their heads?
A. Ice caps!

Q. How do penguins make the perfect pancake?
A. With their flippers!

Q. What do you call fifty penguins at the North Pole?
A. Really lost, because penguins live in the Southern Hemisphere!

Q. Why are penguins good racing drivers?
A. Because they're always in pole position!

Q. How does a penguin build its house?
A. Igloos it together!

Q. Why don't you see penguins in Great Britain?
A. Because they're afraid of Wales!

Q. What do polar bears eat for lunch?
A. Iceburgers!

Q. What's white, furry and shaped like a tooth?
A. A molar bear!

Q. Why do polar bears have fur coats?
A. Because they would look silly in ski jackets!

Q. What weighs two tonnes and rolls around?
A. A walrus on a skateboard!

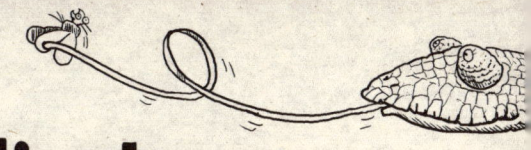

Ridiculous Reptiles

Q. What snake is the best at maths?
A. An adder.

Q. In which river are you sure to find snakes?
A. The Hiss-issippi river!

Q. Did you hear about the snake's love letter?
A. He sealed it with a hiss.

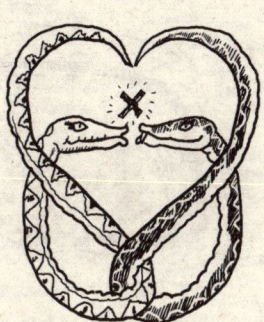

Q. Why did the snake laugh so hard she started to cry?
A. She thought the joke was hiss-terical.

Q. What's the wrong time to reason with a snake?
A. When it's throwing a hissy fit.

Q. Why don't snakes need to weigh themselves?
A. Because they have their own scales.

Q. What kind of snake keeps its car the cleanest?
A. A window viper!

Q. What do two snakes do after they argue?
A. Hiss and make up!

Q. What do snakes use to cut paper?
A. Scissss-ors!

Q. What do you call a snake that builds things?
A. A boa constructor!

Q. What do you call taking a selfie with a rattlesnake?
A. A missss-take.

Q. What is a snake's favourite subject?
A. Hissss-tory!

Q. Why did the turtle cross the road?
A. To get to the shell station!

Q. What kind of photos does a turtle take?
A. Shellfies.

Q. What does a turtle do on its birthday?
A. It shell-ebrates!

Q. What kind of jokes do turtles tell?
A. Absolutely shell-arious ones!

Q. What do you call a turtle that flies?
A. A shell-icopter!

Q. What do you call a truckload of tortoises crashing into a trainload of terrapins?
A. A turtle disaster.

Q. What do turtles use to communicate?
A. A shell-ephone!

Q. What's the most popular name for girl turtles?
A. Shelly.

Q. What's the most popular name for boy turtles?
A. Sheldon.

Q. Why don't crocodiles like fast food?
A. Because they can't catch it!

Q. What do you call a crocodile in a vest?
A. An investigator.

Knock, knock.
Who's there?
Alligator.
Alligator who?
Alligator for her birthday was a card!

Q. What do you call a crocodile with GPS?
A. A navigator.

Q. Why are crocodiles so funny?
A. Their wit is as sharp as their teeth!

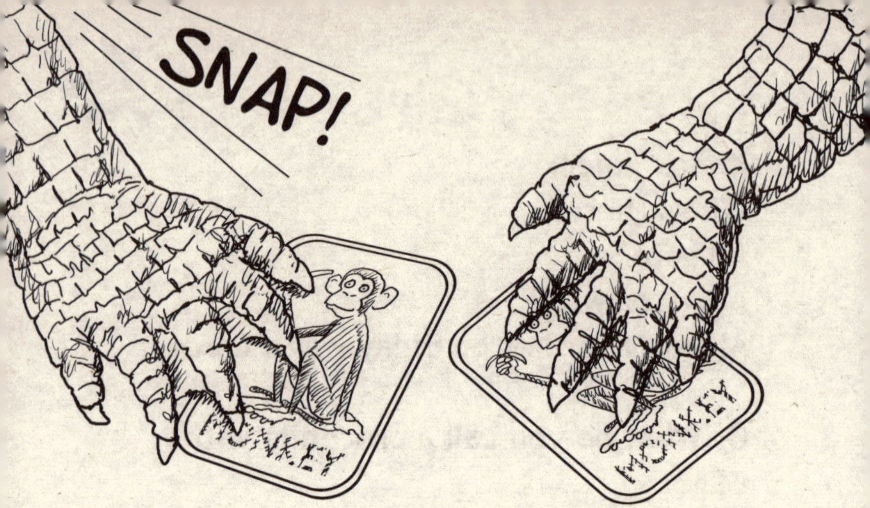

Q. What is a crocodile's favourite card game?
A. Snap.

Q. What do you call a lizard that loves hip hop?
A. A rap-tile!

**Knock, knock.
Who's there?
Iguana.
Iguana who?
Iguana hold your hand!**

Amusing Amphibians

Q. What do you call an amphibian in disguise?
A. Infrognito!

Q. What happens when a frog's car breaks down?
A. He gets toad away.

Q. Where do frogs like to sit?
A. On toadstools.

Q. What does a frog have for lunch?
A. French flies and a diet croak!

Q. Why are frogs so happy?
A. Because they eat everything that bugs them.

Q. What's white on the outside and green on the inside?
A. A frog sandwich!

Q. What do you say to a hitchhiking frog?
A. Hop in!

Q. What does a frog say when he sees something great?
A. Toadly awesome!

Q. Why did the frog croak?
A. Because he ate a poisonous fly!

Q. Why did the frog go to the hospital?
A. He needed a hop-peration!

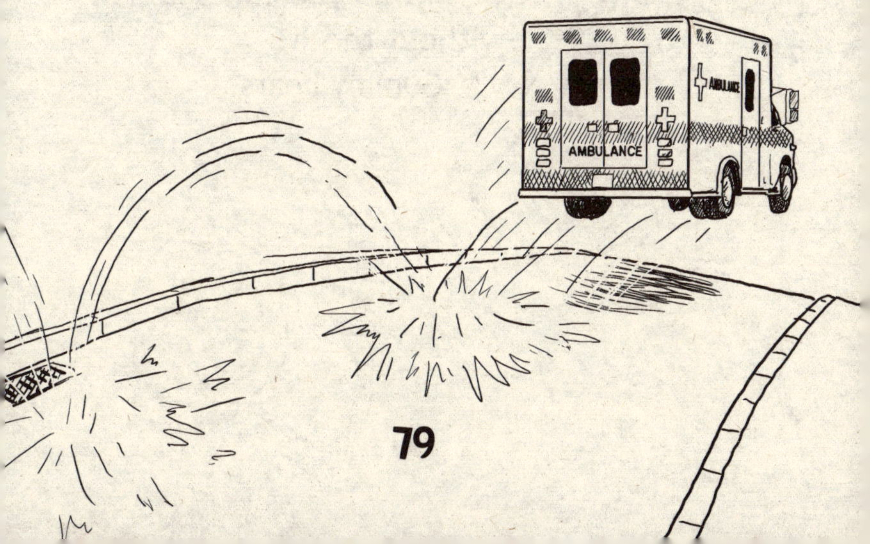

Wacky Woodland

Q. What international sporting event for wild boars is held every four years?
A. The Olym-pigs!

Q. Why didn't the teddy bear eat his lunch?
A. Because he was stuffed!

Q. What do you call bears without ears?
A. Bs.

Q. What do you call bears without teeth?
A. Gummy bears.

Q. Why do badgers like old movies?
A. Because they're in black and white.

**Knock, knock.
Who's there?
Hoo.
Hoo who?
You sound just like an owl!**

Q. What type of books do owls love?
A. Hootdunits!

Q. Why do owls never go on dates in the rain?
A. They find it too wet to woo!

Q. Why do owls like to live in pairs?
A. They don't like to be owl by themselves.

**Knock, knock.
Who's there?
Baby owl.
Baby owl who?
Baby owl see you later.**

Q. What's an owl's favourite party food?
A. Mice cream.

Q. What do you call an owl with a sore throat?
A. A bird that doesn't give a hoot!

Q. What do you call an owl with a low voice?
A. A growl!

Q. Why did the owl, 'owl?
A. Because the woodpecker would peck 'er!

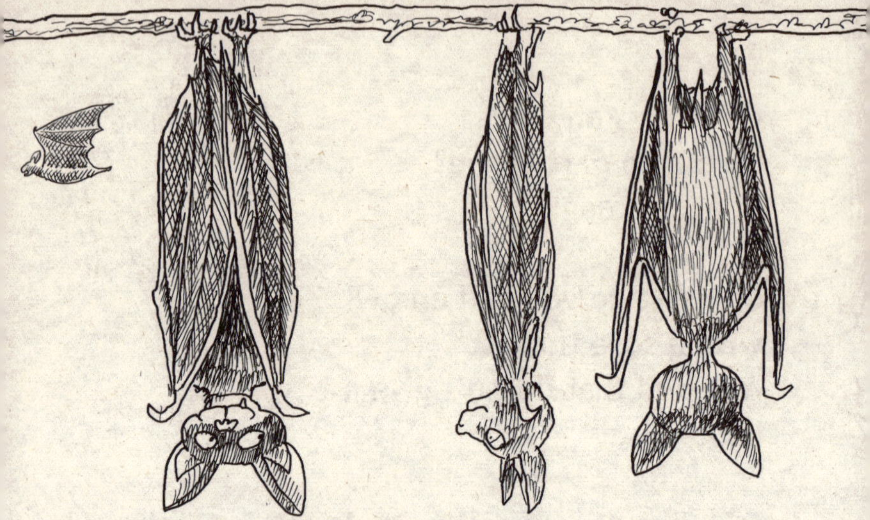

Q. What did the bat say to his friend?
A. Wanna hang out?

Q. What do bats do at night?
A. Aerobatics!

Q. What did the baby mouse say when he saw a bat for the first time?
A. Mummy, I've just seen an angel.

Q. What is the first thing that bats learn at school?
A. The alpha-bat.

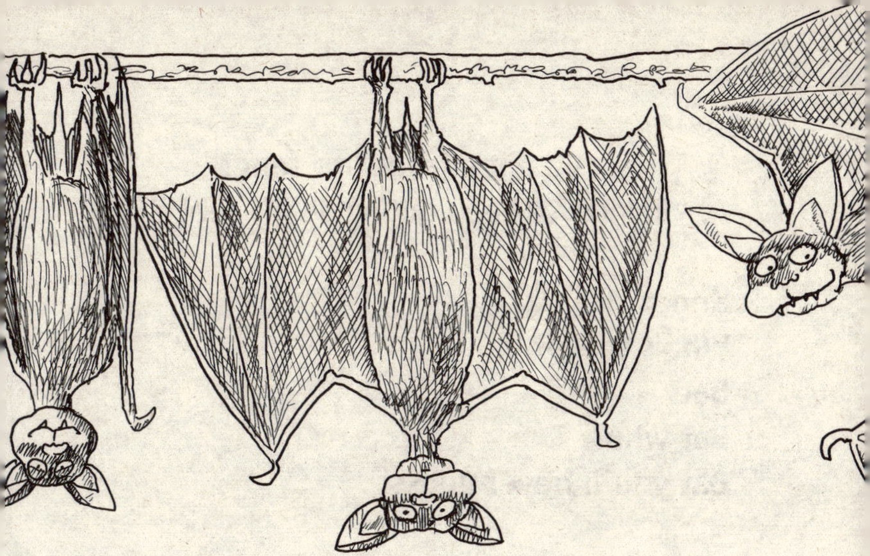

Q. What do you call a bat inside a bell?
A. A dingbat.

Q. How do bats fly without bumping into anything?
A. They use their wing mirrors.

Q. What did the bat say to the vampire?
A. You suck!

Q. What is a bat's favourite song?
A. "Raindrops keep falling on my feet"!

**Knock, knock.
Who's there?
Bat.
Bat who?
Bat you'll never guess!**

Q. Who did Bambi invite to his birthday party?
A. His nearest and deer-est friends.

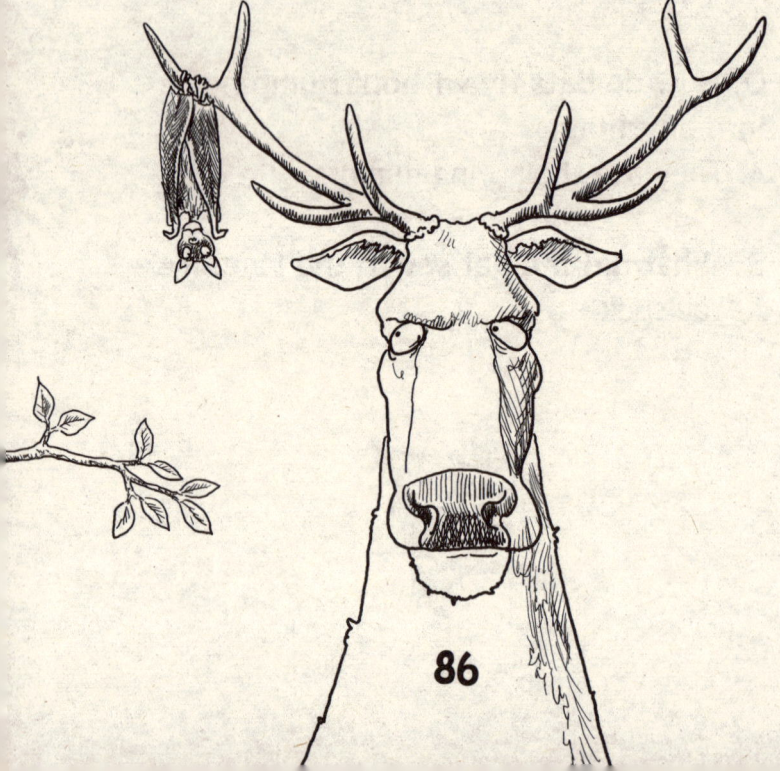

Q. How much is an American deer?
A. Just a buck!

Q. How do you ride a deer?
A. You hang on for deer life.

Q. What do you call a deer with no eyes?
A. I have no i-deer.

Q. Why do male deer need braces?
A. Because they have buckteeth!

Mind-blowing Mash-ups

Q. What do you get if you cross a dog with a cat?
A. An animal that chases itself!

Q. What do you get if you cross a dog with an iguana?
A. A dog that can lick you from the other side of the road!

Q. What do you get if you cross a sheepdog with a rose?
A. A collie-flower!

Q. What do you get if you cross a cat with a lemon?
A. A sourpuss!

Q. What do you get if you cross a cockerel with a poodle?
A. Cockerpoodledoo!

Q. What do you get if you cross a fish with an elephant?
A. Swimming trunks!

Q. What do you get if you cross a dog with a lion?
A. A terrified postman!

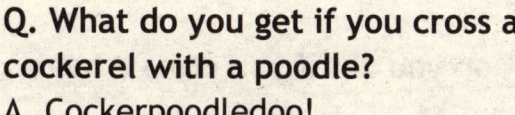

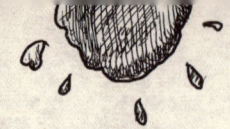

Q. What do you get if you cross a bear with a skunk?
A. Winnie the PHEW!

Q. What do you get if you cross a hedgehog and a giraffe?
A. A three-metre toothbrush.

Q. What do you get if you cross a kangaroo and an elephant?
A. Giant footprints all across Australia!

Q. What do you get if you cross a spider and an elephant?
A. I'm not sure, but if you see one walking on the ceiling then run before it collapses!

Q. What do you get if you cross a cow with a camel?
A. Lumpy milkshakes!

Q. What do you get if you cross a chicken with a dog?
A. Pooched eggs!

Q. What do you get if you cross an octopus and a cow?
A. An animal that can milk itself!

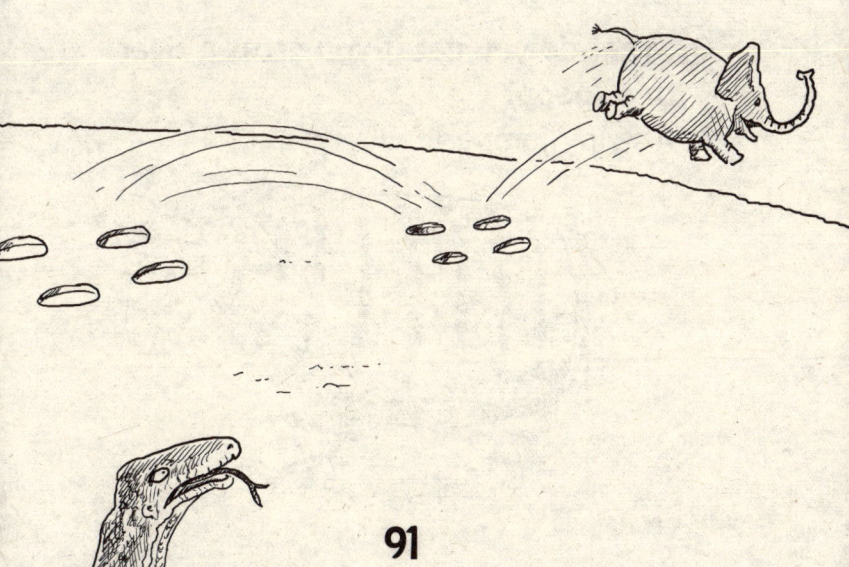

Q. What do you get if you cross a snake with a pie?
A. A pie-thon!

Q. What do you get if you cross some ants with some ticks?
A. All sorts of antics.

Q. What do you get if you cross a rabbit with a leaf blower?
A. A hare dryer!

Q. What do you get if you cross a tiger with a sheep?
A. A stripy jumper!

Q. What do you get if you cross an angry sheep with a moody cow?
A. An animal that's in a baaaad mooood.

Q. What do you get if you cross a sheep with a porcupine?
A. An animal that knits its own socks.

Q. What do you get if you cross a crocodile with a flower?
A. I don't know, but I wouldn't recommend smelling it!

Q. What do you get if you cross a cat with an owl?
A. Meowls.

Q. What do you get if you cross a kangaroo with a sheep?
A. A woolly jumper.

Q. What do you get if you cross a penguin with a zebra?
A. A striped dinner jacket!

Q. What do you get if you cross a chicken with a bell?
A. An alarm cluck.

Q. What do you get if you cross a cow with a goat?
A. A coat!

Q. What do you get when you cross a rabbit with a goat?
A. A hare in your milk!

Q. What do you get when you cross a giraffe with a teacher?
A. A person that everyone looks up to.

Q. What do you get when you cross a crocodile and a rooster?
A. A crocadoodledoo.

Q. What do you get when you cross an owl and an oyster?
A. Pearls of wisdom.

Q. What do you get when you cross a turtle and a porcupine?
A. A slowpoke.

Sporty Jokes

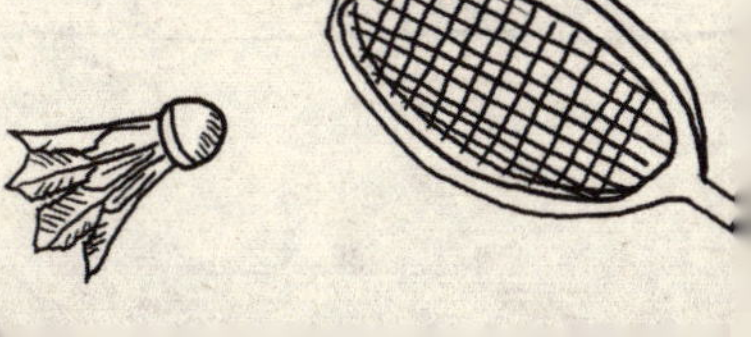

Absurd Athletics

Q. What is harder to catch the faster you run?
A. Your breath!

Q. Why do marathon runners make good students?
A. Because education pays off in the long run!

Q. What is a runner's favourite subject in school?
A. Jog-raphy!

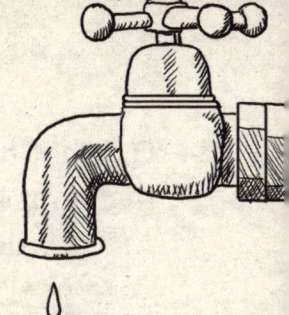

Q. What happened to the world's worst athlete?
A. He ran a bath and came in second!

Q. What do athletes do when they're not running?
A. Surf the sprinternet!

Q. Why don't sprinters listen to music?
A. Because they are always breaking their own records!

Q. Why did the athlete refuse to do the long jump?
A. Because he was short-sighted!

Q. What happened when the two waves had a race?
A. They tide!

Q. Who was the fastest runner of all time?
A. Adam. He was first in the human race!

Q. Why were all the hurdle events cancelled?
A. It wasn't a leap year!

Q. Why did the sprinter bring his barber to the track?
A. Because he wanted to shave a few seconds off his time!

Q. Why did the bald man take up running?
A. He wanted to get some fresh 'air!

Q. What are the two things that could stop you becoming the best athlete in the world?
A. Your feet!

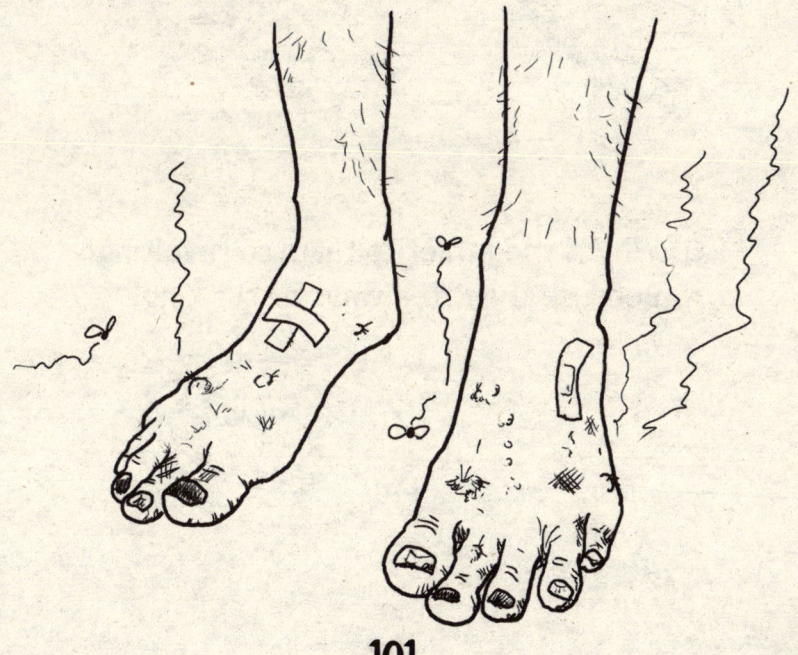

Q. How do you start a jelly race?
A. Get set!

Q. How do you start a firefly race?
A. Ready, steady, glow!

Q. Why is the athletics team so revolting?
A. Because they're always discus-ting!

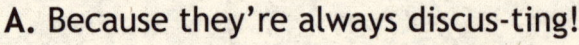

Q. What do you become if you run behind a car?
A. Exhausted!

Q. Did you hear about the marathon runner who ran for three hours but only moved two feet?
A. He only had two feet!

Q. How do you start a teddy bear race?
A. Ready, teddy, go!

Q. What's a banker's favourite Olympic event?
A. Vault!

Q. Who is the most handsome athlete?
A. The sprinter, because he's always dashing!

A woman meets a man carrying a two and a half metre-long metal stick and asks, "Are you a pole vaulter?"
"No," says the man, "I'm German. But how did you know my name is Walter?"

Q. Two silk worms were in a race. Who won?
A. It was a tie!

Q. What happened to the marathon runner whose shoes were too small?
A. She suffered the agony of defeat!

Q. What happened when a tap, a lettuce and a tomato had a race?
A. The tap was running, the lettuce was a head and the tomato couldn't ketchup!

Archery Antics

Q. What kind of bow can't be tied?
A. A crossbow!

Q. What is it called when two archers score the same?
A. A bowtie!

Q. Why did the arrow-maker get sacked?
A. He was missing the point!

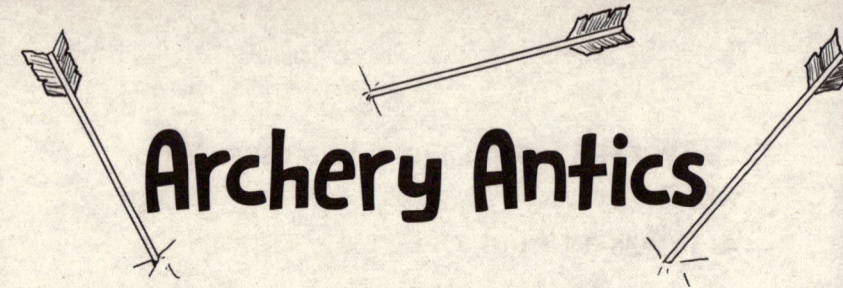

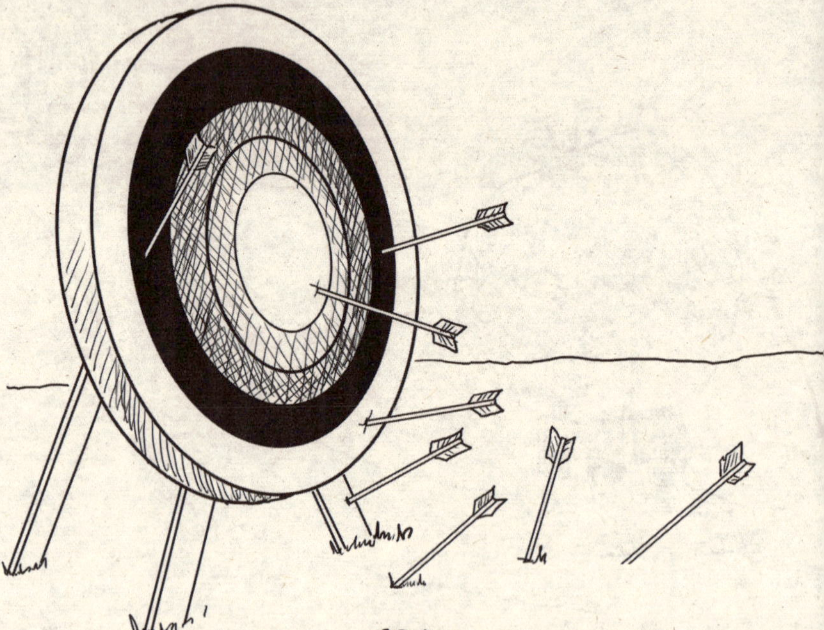

Q. What did the archer say when she nearly got shot at an archery contest?
A. Wow, that was an arrow escape!

Q. Did you hear about the archer who shot an arrow into the air?
A. He missed!

Q. What did the archer get when he hit a bullseye?
A. A very angry bull!

Q. How does an archer tie his shoelaces?
A. With a long bow!

Q. What do you get when you cross an archer with a gift-wrapper?
A. Ribbon Hood!

Q. Why did the man find archery too frustrating?
A. Because it has so many drawbacks!

Badminton Buffoonery

Q. What is Count Dracula's favourite sport?
A. Bat-minton!

Q. What did the shuttlecock say when it got hit?
A. Who's making all that racquet?

Q. What's a sheep's favourite game?
A. Baa-dminton!

Tom: Why did the badminton player go to prison?
Tim: Because he was a bad man, Tom!

Q. What do you call a bald man in a wedding dress?
A. A shuttlecock!

Q. How do hens encourage their favourite badminton players?
A. They egg them on!

Barmy Basketball

Q. Why are basketball players messy eaters?
A. They're always dribbling!

Q. What do you get if you cross a basketball with a newborn snake?
A. A bouncing baby boa!

Q. Why can't you play basketball with pigs?
A. They always hog the ball!

Q. Why was Cinderella such a bad basketball player?
A. Her coach was a pumpkin!

Q. What do you call an unbelievable story about a basketball player?
A. A tall tale!

Q. What's the difference between a dog and a basketball player?
A. One drools and the other dribbles!

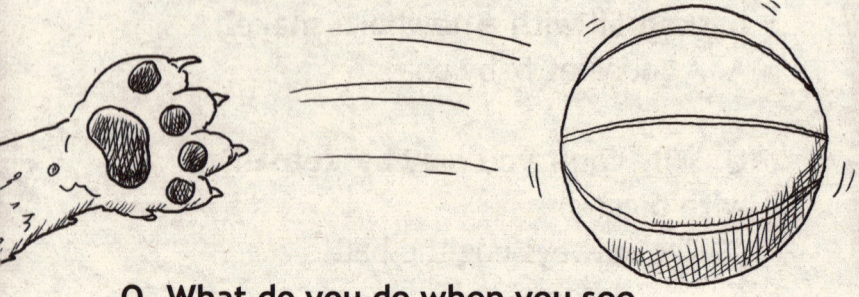

Q. What do you do when you see an elephant with a basketball?
A. Get out of the way!

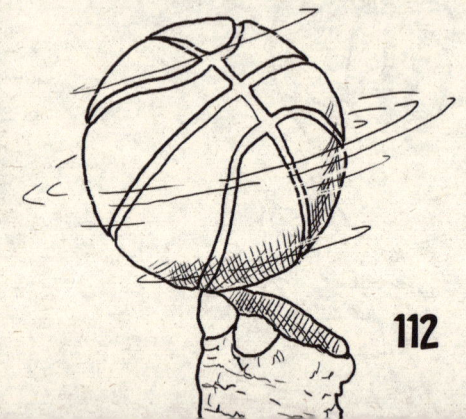

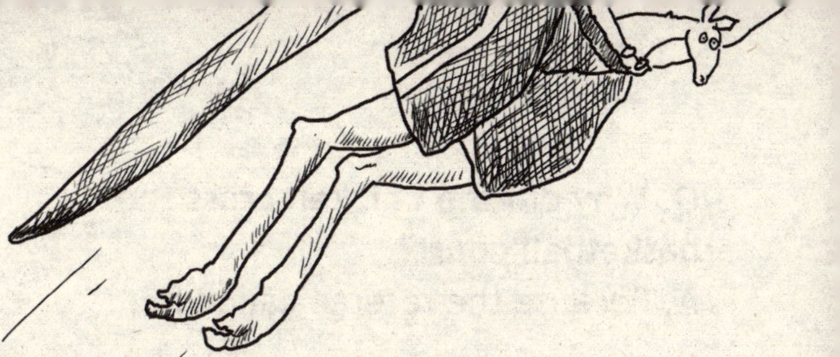

Q. Why was the kangaroo invited to join the basketball team?
A. He was good at jump shots!

Q. Why did the basketball player go to jail?
A. Because he shot the ball!

Q. Why do basketball players love doughnuts?
A. Because they can dunk them!

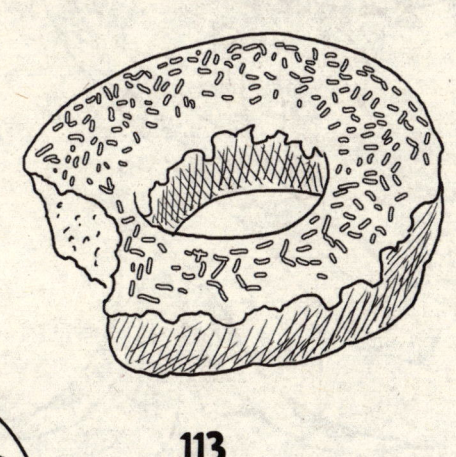

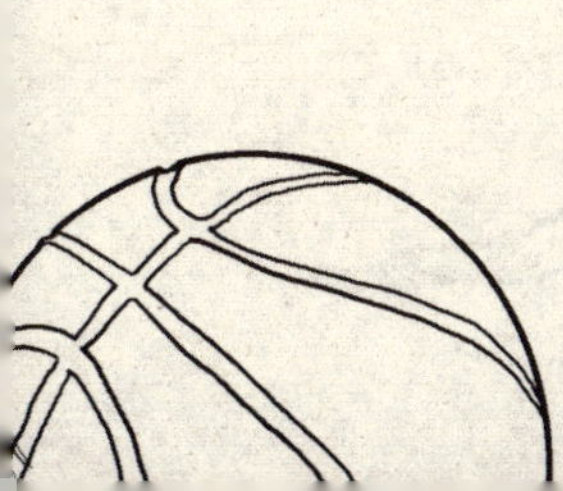

Q. Why did the chicken cross the basketball court?
A. Because the referee called foul!

Q. How do you play basketball in Hawaii?
A. With hula-hoops!

1st sports fan: I hear they are feeding the basketball players bananas before each game.
2nd sports fan: Does it make them shoot any better?
1st sports fan: No. But it makes the game more a-peel-ing!

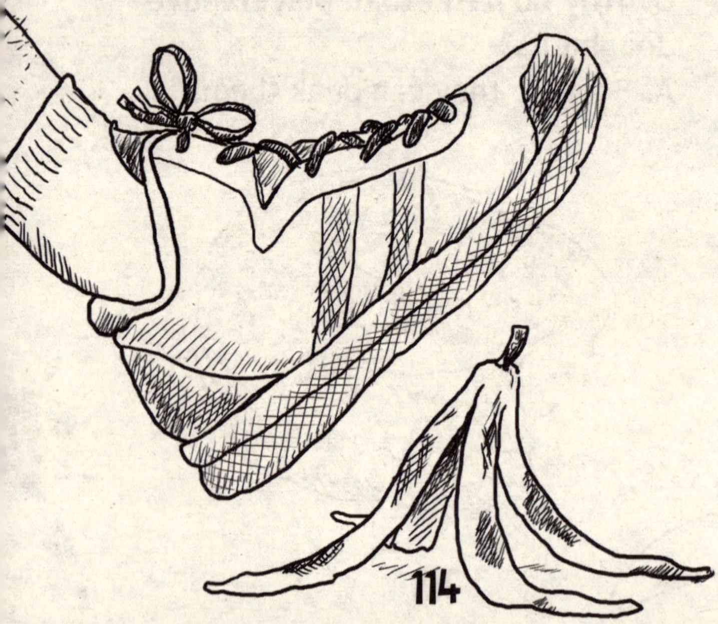

1st basketball player: We're going to win this game – don't you think?
2nd basketball player: I certainly hoop so!

Q. Why did the old basketball player become a judge?
A. He wanted to stay on the court!

Q. Why were the chicken, turkey, pheasant and goose allowed on the basketball court, but not the duck?
A. Because at a basketball game, five fouls and you're out!

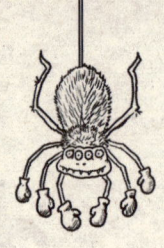

Boisterous Boxing

Q. When do boxers start wearing gloves?
A. When it gets cold!

Q. What ring is square?
A. A boxing ring!

Q. How did the featherweight boxer win all his fights?
A. He tickled his opponents!

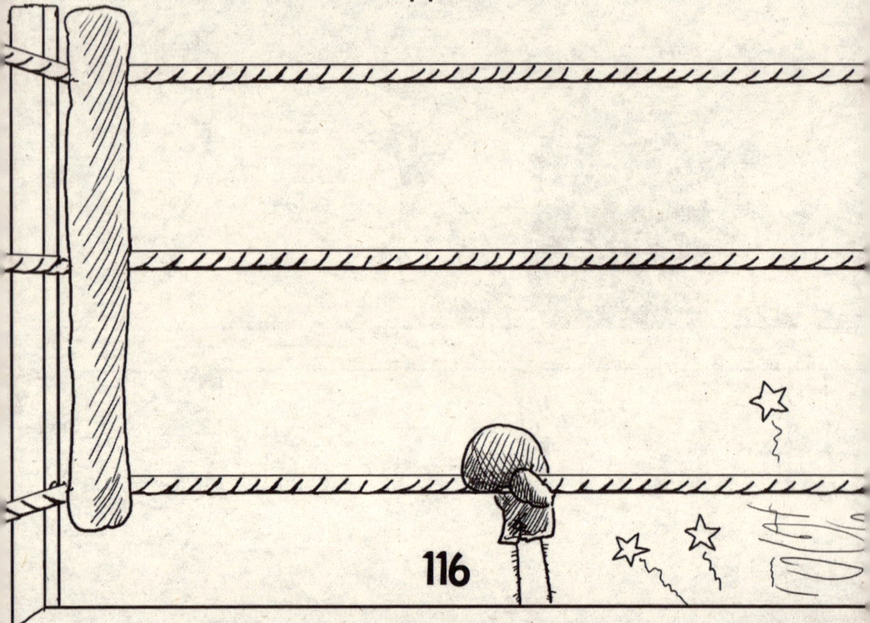

Q. What is the best part of a boxer's joke?
A. The punch line!

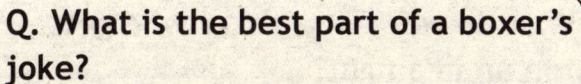

Q. How do you make a fruit punch?
A. Give it boxing lessons!

Q. What does a boxer ask for at the hairdresser?
A. An uppercut!

Q. What is the difference between a boxer and a man with a cold?
A. One knows his blows and the other blows his nose!

Q. What do you call a boxer who gets beaten up in a fight?
A. A sore loser!

Q. What's the difference between a nail and a boxer?
A. One's knocked in and the other's knocked out!

Q. Does a match box?
A. No, but a tin can!

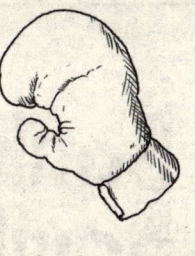

**Knock, knock.
Who's there?
Raoul.
Raoul who?
Raoul with the punches!**

**Q. What happened when Santa took up boxing?
A. He decked the halls!**

**Q. Why did the boxer wear gloves to bed?
A. Because he wanted to hit the sack!**

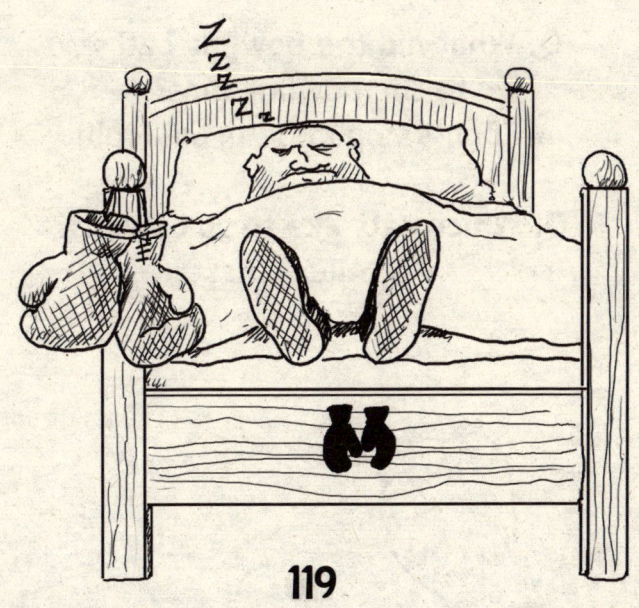

Bonkers Bowling

Q. What is the world's quietest sport?
A. Bowling, because you can hear a pin drop!

Q. What did the bowling ball say to the bowling pins?
A. Don't stop me, I'm on a roll!

Q. Which cats like to go bowling?
A. Alley cats!

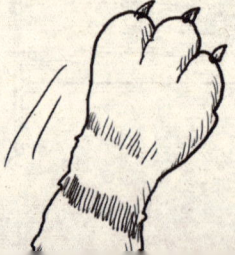

Bowler 1: I was asked to leave the bowling team after I knocked all the pins down in one go.
Bowler 2: That doesn't seem fair!
Bowler 1: The pins were in the next alley!

Q. What should you do with old bowling balls?
A. Give them to elephants to use as marbles!

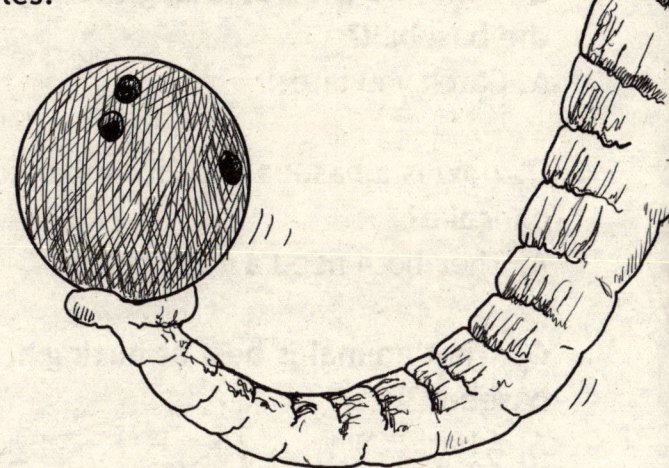

Q. What happened to the girl who took her knitting to the bowling alley?
A. She got pins and needles!

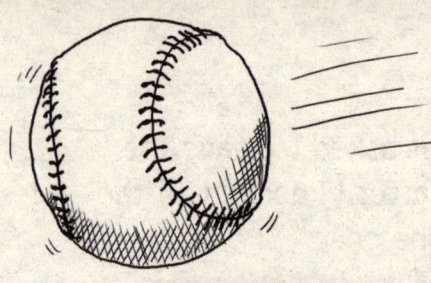

Brilliant Baseball

Q. What did the baseball glove say to the baseball?
A. Catch you later!

Q. How is a baseball team similar to a pancake?
A. They both need a good batter!

Q. What animal is best at hitting a baseball?
A. A bat!

Q. How do baseball players stay cool?
A. They sit next to the fans!

Q. Why are baseball players so rich?
A. Because they play on diamonds!

Q. Why are criminals great baseball players?
A. Because they already know how to hit, run and steal!

Q. What goes all the way around a baseball field but never moves?
A. The fence!

Comic Cricket

Q. When is cricket a crime?
A. When there's a hit and run!

Q. Why can't Robin play cricket?
A. Because he's lost his bat, man!

Q. How do you stop moles digging up the cricket pitch?
A. Hide their spades!

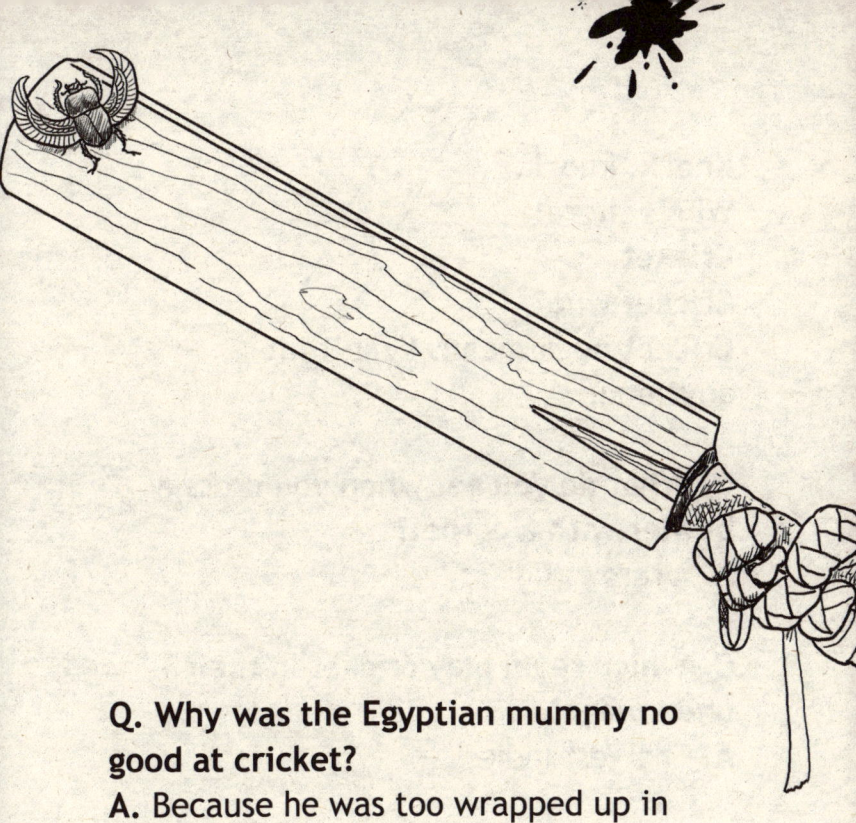

Q. Why was the Egyptian mummy no good at cricket?
A. Because he was too wrapped up in himself!

Q. What did the cricket pitch say to the player?
A. I hate it when people treat me like dirt!

Q. Why did the vampires cancel the cricket game?
A. Because they couldn't find their bats!

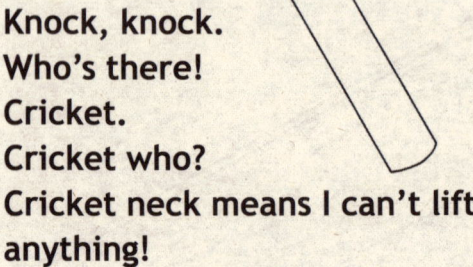

Knock, knock.
Who's there!
Cricket.
Cricket who?
Cricket neck means I can't lift anything!

Q. What do you get when you cross a bowler with a carpet?
A. A throw rug!

Q. Which team play cricket in their underwear?
A. The Vest Indies!

Q. What is an insect's favourite sport?
A. Cricket!

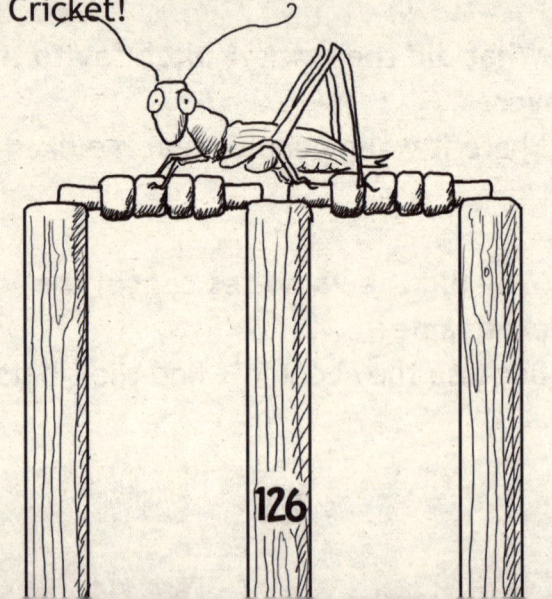

Cycling Capers

Q. Why couldn't the bicycle stand up?
A. Because it was two tyred!

Knock, knock.
Who's there?
Isabelle.
Isabelle who?
Isabelle necessary on a bicycle?

Q. What's the hardest part of learning to ride a bike?
A. The pavement!

Q. What do you get if you cross a bike and a flower?
A. Bicycle petals!

Q. What do you call a bicycle built by a chemist?
A. Bike-carbonate of soda!

Q. When is a bicycle not a bicycle?
A. When it turns into a driveway!

Q. Why don't bankers make good cyclists?
A. They tend to lose their balance!

Q. What does a racing bike call its dad?
A. Pop-cycle!

Q. How do angry cyclists travel through the forest?
A. They take the psycho path!

Q. What's big, scary and has three wheels?
A. A monster riding a tricycle!

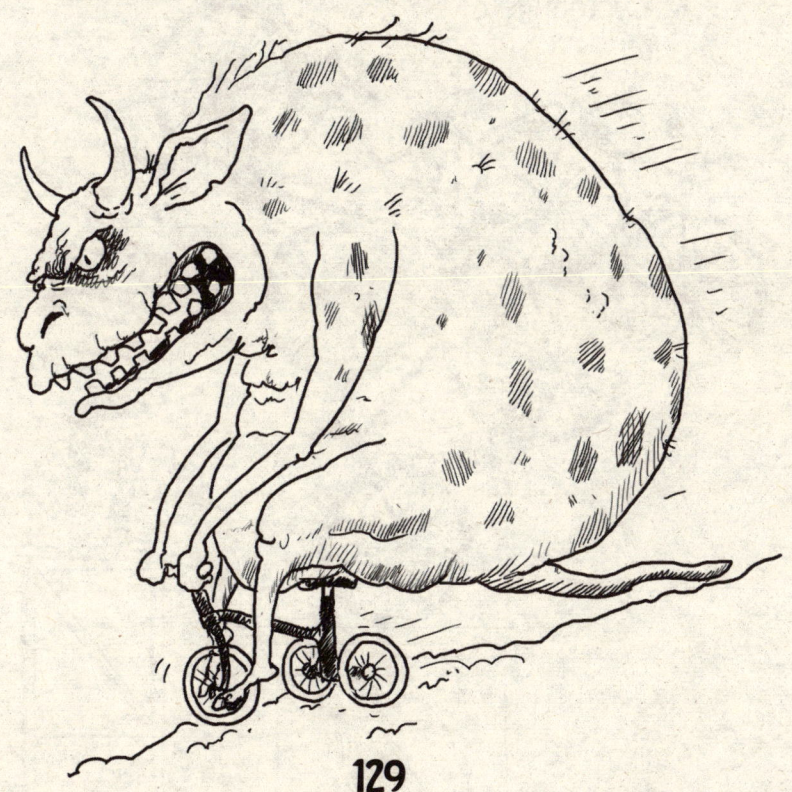

Q. Why did the little boy take his bicycle to bed with him?
A. Because he didn't want to walk in his sleep!

Q. What is a ghost-proof bicycle?
A. One with no spooks in it!

Q. What do you call an artist who sculpts with bicycle parts?
A. Cycleangelo!

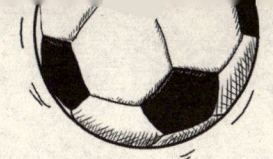

Funny Football

Q. What do you call it when T-Rex scores a goal?
A. A dino-score!

Q. How did the football pitch end up as triangle?
A. Somebody took a corner!

Q. What is a ghost's favourite position in football?
A. Ghoul keeper!

Q. What do footballers and magicians have in common?
A. They both do hat tricks!

Q. Which goalkeeper can jump higher than a crossbar?
A. All of them, a crossbar can't jump!

Q. What did the footballer say to the football?
A. I get a kick out of you!

Q. Why do artists never win at football?
A. Because they keep drawing!

Q. What type of football players do bank managers like the most?
A. Goalkeepers, because they are the best savers!

Q. What is a footballer's favourite drink?
A. Penal-tea!

Q. Where do footballers go to dance?
A. The foot-ball!

Q. What did the left football boot say to the right football boot?
A. Between us we should have a ball!

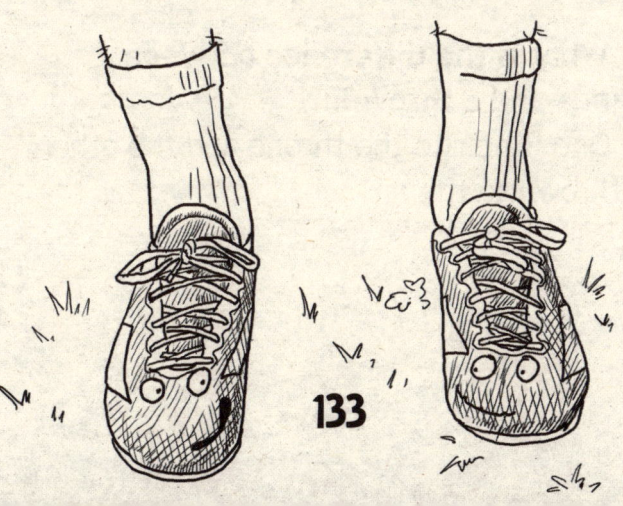

Q. What did the bumblebee striker say?
A. Hi've scored!

Q. Which insect is useless in goal?
A. A fumble bee!

Q. When is a football player like a grandfather clock?
A. When he is a striker!

Q. What is the difference between a prince and a throw-in?
A. One is heir to the throne and the other is thrown to the air!

CHANGING ROOM

Q. What part of a football pitch smells nicest?
A. The scenter spot!

Q. What did the footballer say when he accidentally burped during a game?
A. Sorry, it was a freak hic!

Q. What part of a football stadium never stays the same?
A. The changing rooms!

Q. Why were two football managers sketching china before the start of the game?
A. It was the cup draw!

Q. Why should you be careful playing football against a team of big cats?
A. They might be cheetahs!

Q. What should a football team do if the pitch is flooded?
A. Bring on their subs!

Q. What do you call a girl who stands inside goalposts and stops the ball rolling away?
A. Annette!

Q. What ship holds 20 football teams but only three leave it each season?
A. The Premier-ship!

Q. Which football side did Shy Barry and Very Quiet Vernon play for?
A. The reserve-d team!

Q. Why did the football quit the team?
A. It was tired of being kicked around!

Q. What spins around and around and chants 'Here we go, here we go, here we go!'
A. A football fan!

Q. Why were football fans once like old cars?
A. They never went anywhere without a rattle!

Q. What is a snake's favourite football team?
A. Slitherpool!

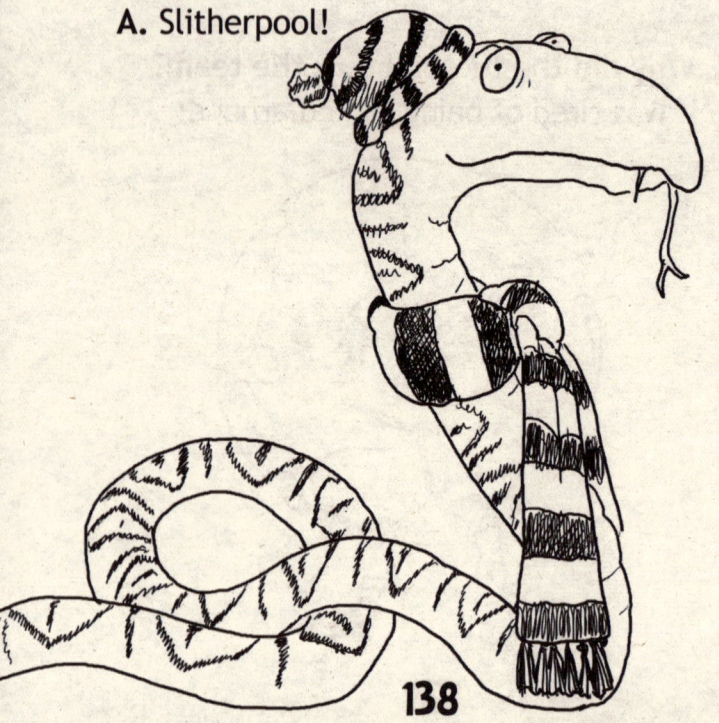

Q. What is pink, has four legs and plays football?
A. Queens Pork Rangers!

Q. What do you call a football team crossed with ice cream?
A. Aston Vanilla!

Q. What do earwigs sing at football matches?
A. 'Earwig-o, Earwig-o, Earwig-o!'

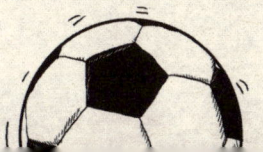

Q. What is a striker's favourite song?
A. Shake, rattle and goal!

Q. Why is Dracula a hopeless goalkeeper?
A. He hates crosses!

Q. What is a goalkeeper's favourite lunch?
A. Beans on post!

Q. Why do ghosts go to football matches?
A. So they can boo the referee!

Q. Why did the goalpost get angry?
A. Because the bar was rattled!

Q. What runs along the edge of the pitch but never moves?
A. The sideline!

Q. What has 22 legs and two wings but can't fly?
A. A football team!

Goofy Golf

Q. Why did the golfer have an extra pair of trousers?
A. In case he got a hole in one!

Q. Why did Tarzan spend so much time on the golf course?
A. He was perfecting his swing!

Q. Why type of top should you wear while golfing?
A. A tee-shirt!

Q. What's a golfer's favourite letter?
A. Tee!

Q. When is the best time to play golf?
A. Tee-time!

Q. What goes putt-putt-putt-putt-putt-putt?
A. A really bad golfer!

Golfer: Do you think my game is improving?
Caddy: Yes, sir. You miss the ball much closer now.

Q. Where did the rock star go to play golf?
A. Pebble beach!

Q. How many golfers does it take to change a light bulb?
A. Fore!

Golfer: This is the worst course I've ever played on.
Caddy: This isn't the golf course. We left that an hour ago.

Golfer: Do you like my game?
Caddy: Very good, sir! But personally I prefer golf.

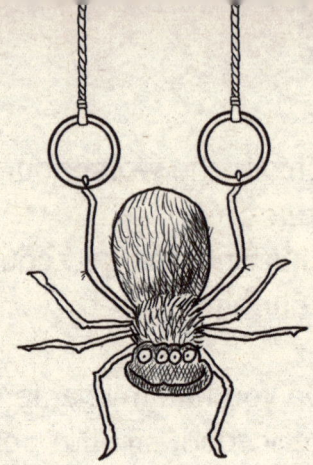

Gymnastics Gags

Q. What do bananas do best in gymnastics?
A. The splits!

Q. What did the Egyptian mummy coach say at the end of gymnastics practice?
A. Let's wrap this up!

Q. Why shouldn't you pick on a gymnast?
A. You never know when they might flip!

Q. Why did the gymnasts get married?
A. Because they were head over heels in love!

Q. Why do gymnasts make great friends?
A. They'll always do you a good turn and will bend over backwards to help!

Q. Why was the gymnast waving her bank statements in the air?
A. She wanted to display her great balance!

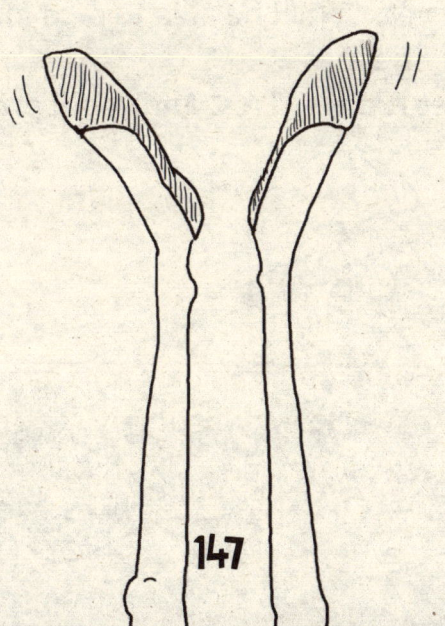

Hilarious Horse Racing

Q. What's a racehorse's favourite TV show?
A. Neighbours!

Q. Which side of a racehorse has more hair?
A. The outside!

A racehorse owner takes his sick horse to the vet. "Will I be able to race him again?" he asks.
The vet replies, "Yes! And you'll probably win!"

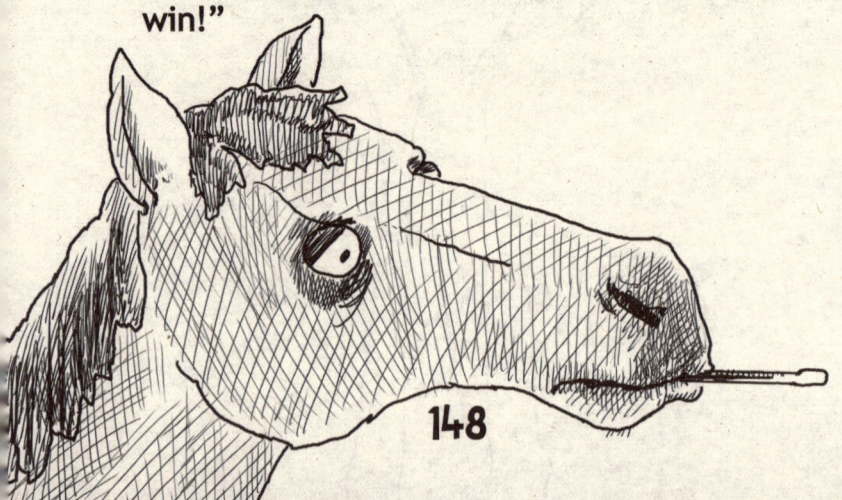

Q. Why should you never be rude to a jump jockey?
A. In case he takes offence (a fence)!

Q. Did you hear about the racehorse that got a job in a watch factory?
A. All he did was stand around making faces!

Q. What happened when the racehorse ran with an apple in his mouth?
A. He was pipped at the post!

Q. What do racehorses like to eat?
A. Fast food!

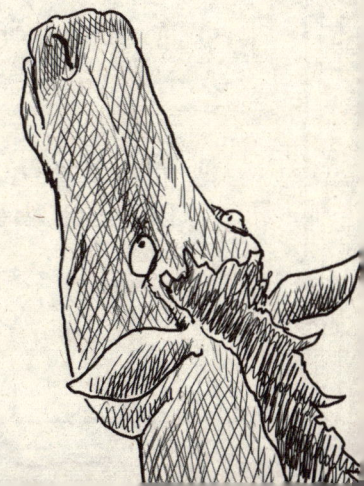

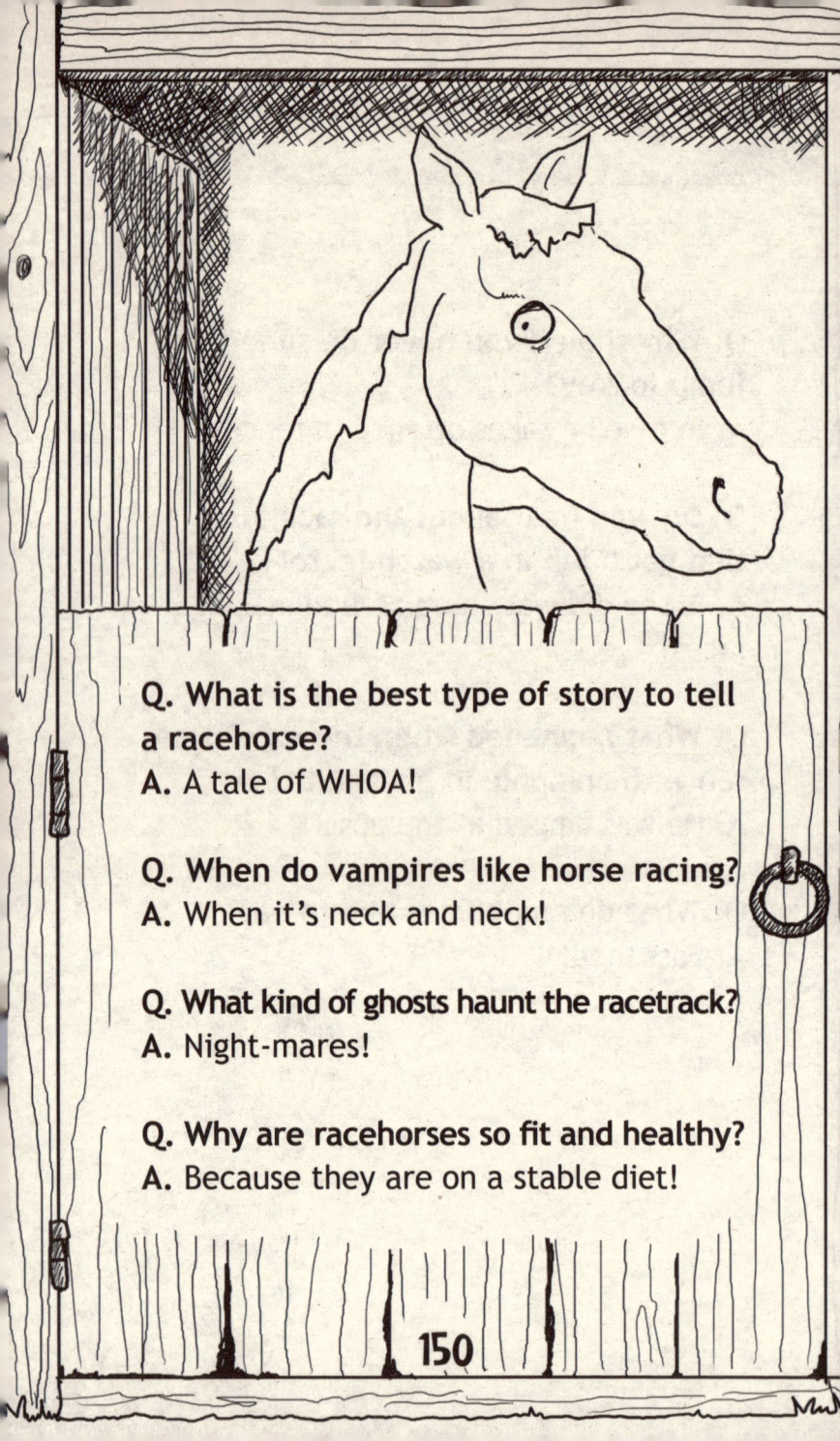

Q. What is the best type of story to tell a racehorse?
A. A tale of WHOA!

Q. When do vampires like horse racing?
A. When it's neck and neck!

Q. What kind of ghosts haunt the racetrack?
A. Night-mares!

Q. Why are racehorses so fit and healthy?
A. Because they are on a stable diet!

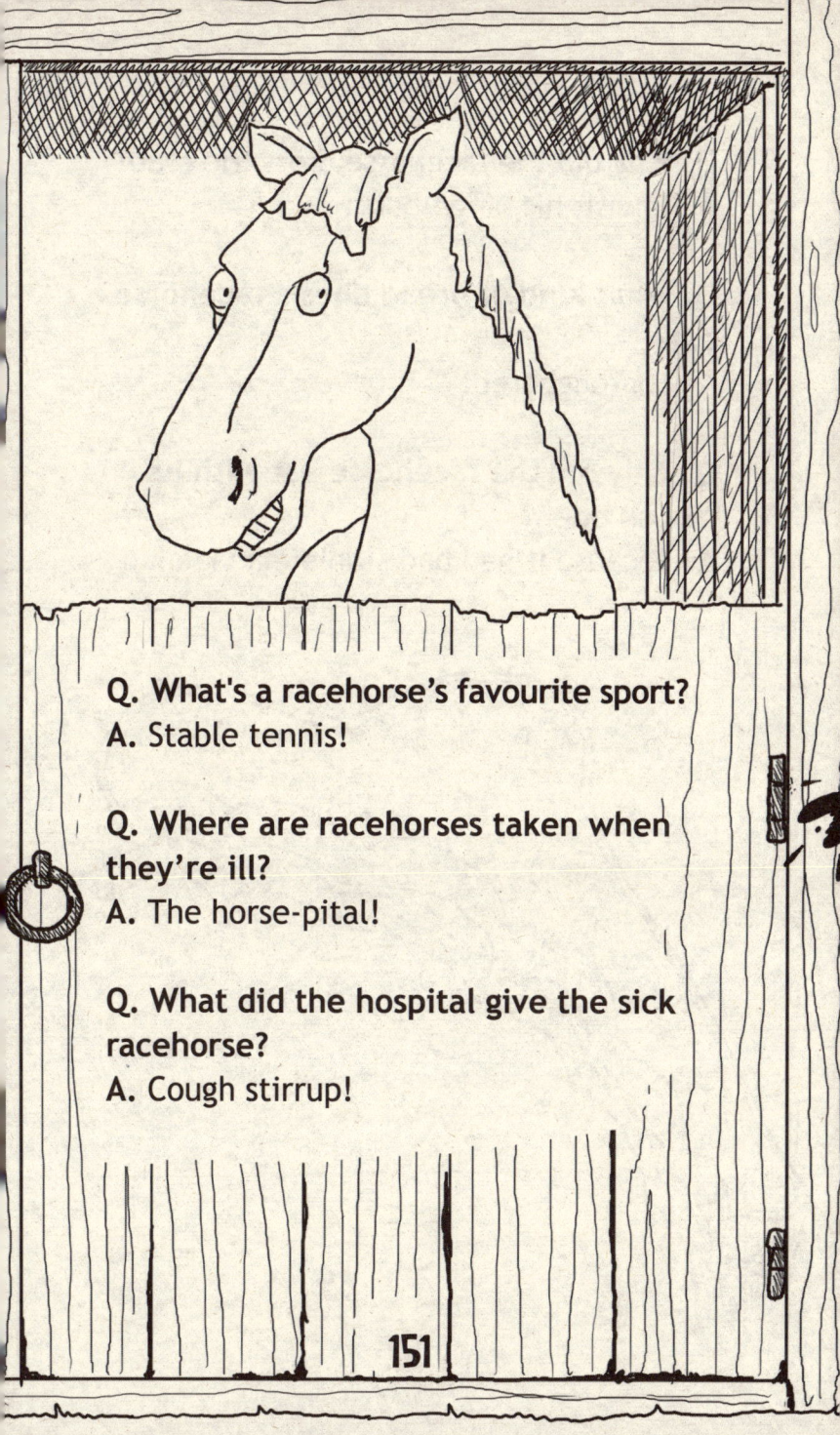

Q. What's a racehorse's favourite sport?
A. Stable tennis!

Q. Where are racehorses taken when they're ill?
A. The horse-pital!

Q. What did the hospital give the sick racehorse?
A. Cough stirrup!

Q. Why did the racehorse cross the road?
A. To visit his *neigh*-bour!

Q. What kind of bread does a racehorse eat?
A. Thoroughbred!

Q. Why did the racehorse eat with its mouth open?
A. Because it had bad stable manners!

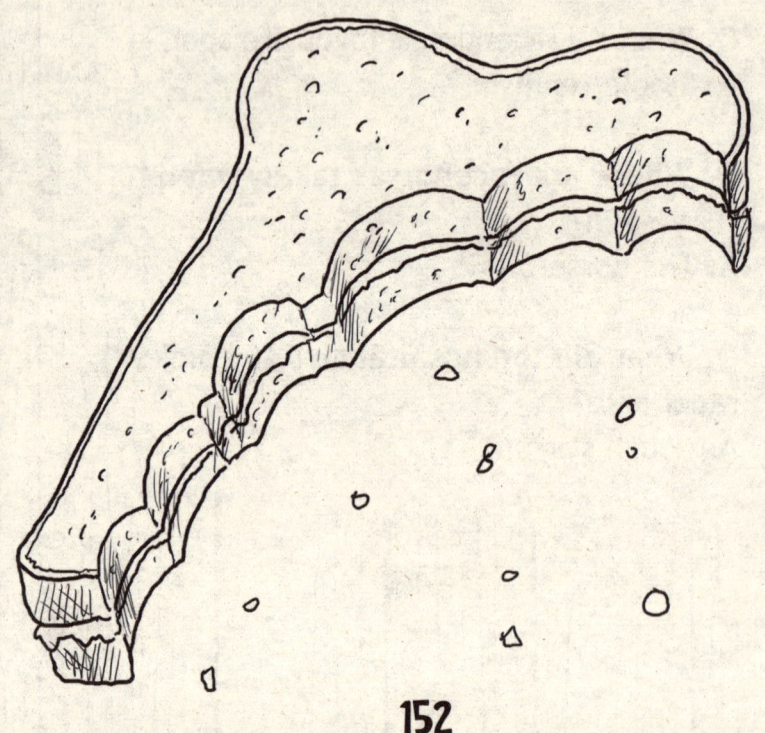

Q. How do you know when a racehorse is really slow?
A. The jockey keeps a diary of his trip around the racecourse!

Q. Why did the jockey stand behind the horse?
A. He thought he might get a kick out of it!

Q. What is the difference between a racehorse and a duck?
A. One goes quick and the other goes quack!

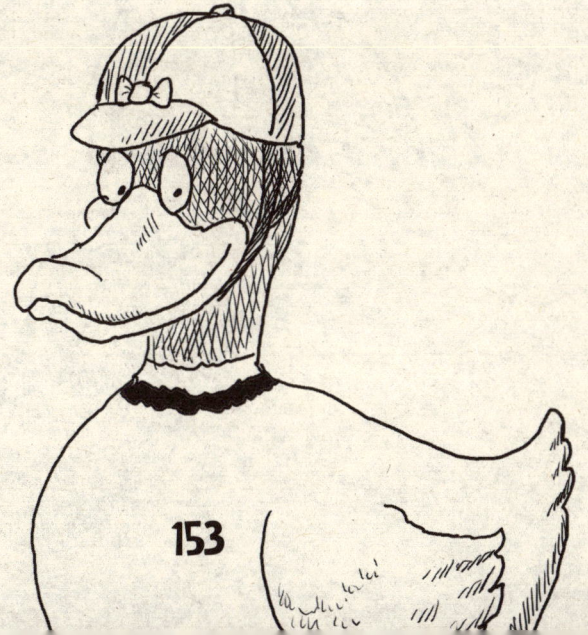

Q. What did the horse say when he fell over?
A. I can't giddy-up!

Q. What do you say to an impatient jockey?
A. Hold your horses!

Q. What is the difference between a racehorse and the weather?
A. One is reined up, the other rains down!

Hysterical Hockey

Q. What helps ghosts to win hockey matches?
A. Their team spirit!

Q. Why couldn't the car play hockey?
A. Because it only had one boot!

Q. Why couldn't the pig play hockey?
A. Because he had pulled his hamstring!

Q. Why did the chicken get sent off?
A. For persistent fowl play!

Q. What happens if it rains and rains and the hockey pitch is knee-deep in water?
A. They turn on the floodlights!

Q. What did the hockey coach say to the player who lost the ball?
A. Find it quickly or I'll give you some stick!

Q. Did you hear about the two flies playing hockey in a saucer?
A. They were practising for the cup!

Q. How do you stop squirrels playing hockey in the garden?
A. Hide the ball - it drives them nuts!

Incredible Ice Skating

Q. What did the ice skater say to the ice when she slipped?
A. I'm gonna let it slide this time!

Q. How is music like ice skating?
A. If you don't 'C sharp' you'll 'B flat'!

Q. How long does it take to learn to ice skate?
A. A few sittings!

Q. Why is it dangerous to tell a joke while ice skating?
A. Because the ice might crack up!

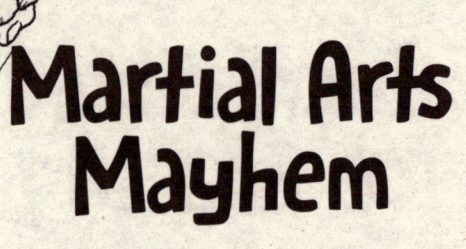
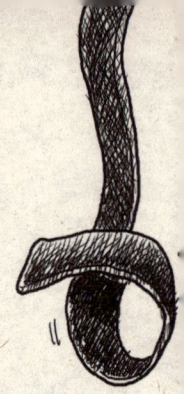

Martial Arts Mayhem

Q. Which martial art do vegetarians study?
A. Kung-Tofu!

Q. Why don't karate experts salute?
A. They might hurt their heads!

Q. Why didn't the skeleton go to judo?
A. He had no body to go with!

Q. Why is the skeleton afraid to do karate?
A. Because he doesn't have any guts!

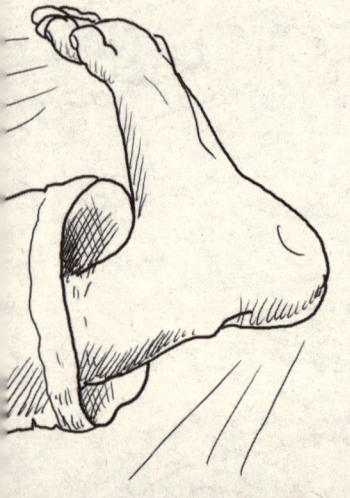
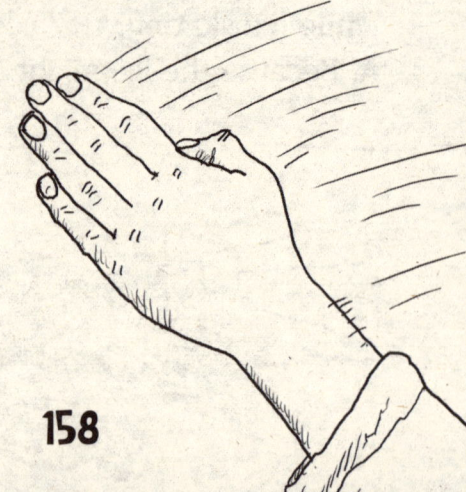

Q. What do Chinese wrestlers have for breakfast?
A. Kung food!

Q. Did you hear about the new karate video?
A. It became a hit and a blockbuster!

Q. Why did the karate expert wear a black belt?
A. To keep his trousers up!

Q. What do you call a pig that does karate?
A. A pork chop!

Ridiculous Rugby

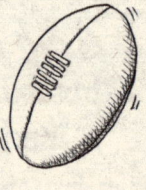

Q. Why are rugby players so persistent?
A. They are always willing to give it one last try!

Q. Why did the rugby player go to see the vet?
A. Because his calves were hurting!

Q. What's a bee's favourite sport?
A. Rug-bee!

Q. Why aren't rugby stadiums built in outer space?
A. Because there is no atmosphere!

Q. What trees can't you climb at a rugby ground?
A. The lavatories!

A rugby player went to the doctor: "When I got back from the game I found that when I touched my legs, my arms, my head, my tummy and everywhere else, it really hurt".
The doctor said: "You've broken your finger".

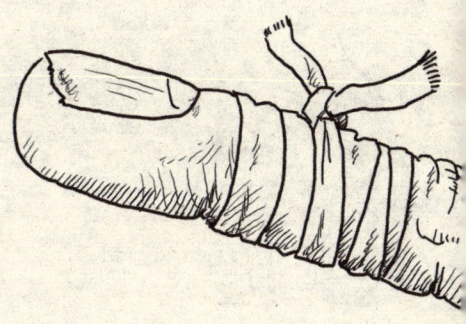

Q. What lights up a rugby stadium?
A. A rugby match!

Side-Splitting Swimming

Q. Why did the man keep doing backstroke?
A. Because he had just eaten and didn't want to swim on a full stomach!

Q. Why can't two elephants go swimming together?
A. Because they only have one pair of trunks between them!

Q. When is your swimming costume like a bell?
A. When you wring it out!

Q. How can you swim a mile in just a few seconds?
A. Swim over a waterfall!

Q. Where do zombies go swimming?
A. The Dead Sea!

Q. Where do ghosts like to go swimming?
A. Lake Eerie!

Q. What kind of swimming stroke can you use on toast?
A. BUTTER-fly!

Q. What is a polar bear's favourite stroke?
A. Blubber-fly!

Q. How do people swimming in the ocean say hi to each other?
A. They wave!

Q. In which direction does a chicken swim?
A. Cluck-wise!

Q. What word looks the same backwards and upside down?
A. SWIMS

Q. Which kind of exercises are best for a swimmer?
A. Pool-ups!

Q. What stroke do sheep enjoy doing?
A. The *baaaa*ckstroke!

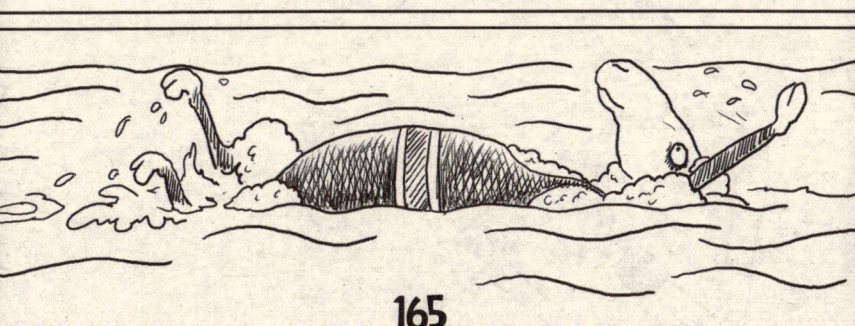

Silly Sailing

Q. What is a sailor's favourite snack?
A. Chocolate ship cookies!

Q. Why do sailors always carry bags of dried fruit?
A. In case they get into trouble, the currants could carry them ashore!

Q. What day is the best to go sailing?
A. Winds-day!

Q. Why can't you build a fire in a kayak?
A. You can't have your kayak and heat it!

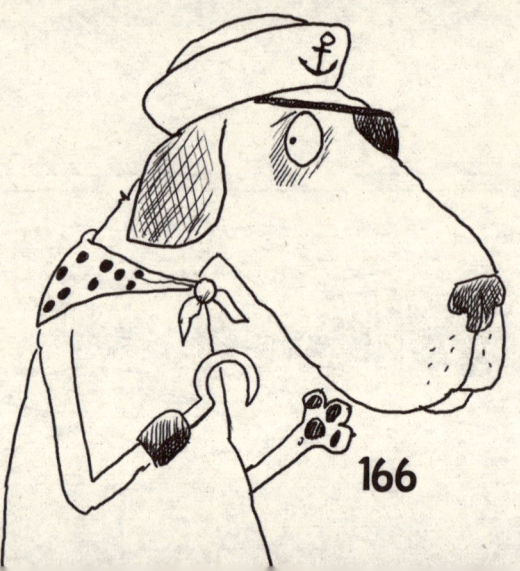

Knock, knock.
Who's there?
Canoe.
Canoe who?
Canoe come out and play?

Q. Why did the boy take his skipping rope onto the ship?
A. He wanted to become the skipper!

Q. What happens when sailing boats get really old?
A. They keel over!

Q. What do sailors put on their soup?
A. Crew-tons!

Q. Why did the captain lose the yacht race?
A. He found himself in a no-wind situation!

Q. How do retired sailors greet each other?
A. Long time, no sea!

Q. How does a boat show affection?
A. It hugs the shore!

Q. How do sailors get their clothes clean?
A. They throw them overboard and they wash ashore!

Spectacular Sports Day

Q. Why don't eggs enjoy the egg-and-spoon race?
A. They can't take a yolk!

Q. Did you hear about the two men who ran in the fathers' race at sports day?
A. One ran in short bursts, the other in burst shorts!

Q. What happened to the boy with a fear of hurdles?
A. He got over it!

Q. Why did the school's best athlete lose the decathlon?
A. She had a slipped discus!

Q. Why did the boy come first in the 100-metre sprint?
A. He had athlete's foot!

Q. Who is the school's shot put champion?
A. Eva Brick!

Q. What has eleven heads and runs around screaming?
A. A school hockey team!

Q. Why did the boy turn up to sports day with some barbed wire under his arm?
A. He thought he'd try his luck at fencing!

Q. What do long-distance runners do when they forget something?
A. They jog their memory!

Q. What has 22 legs and goes "crunch, crunch, crunch!"
A. The school football team eating crisps!

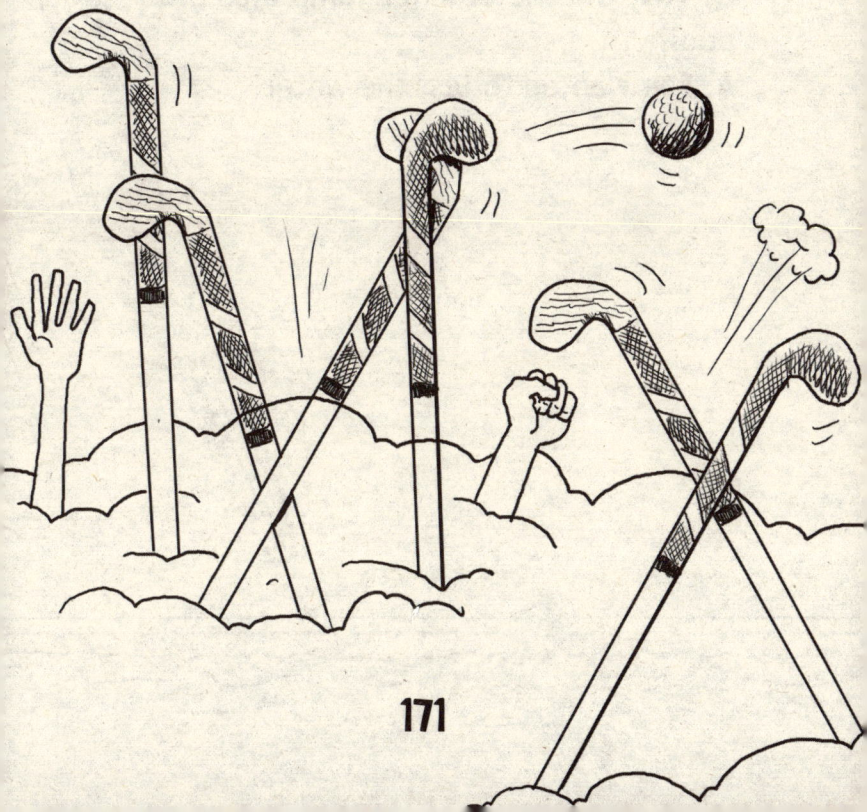

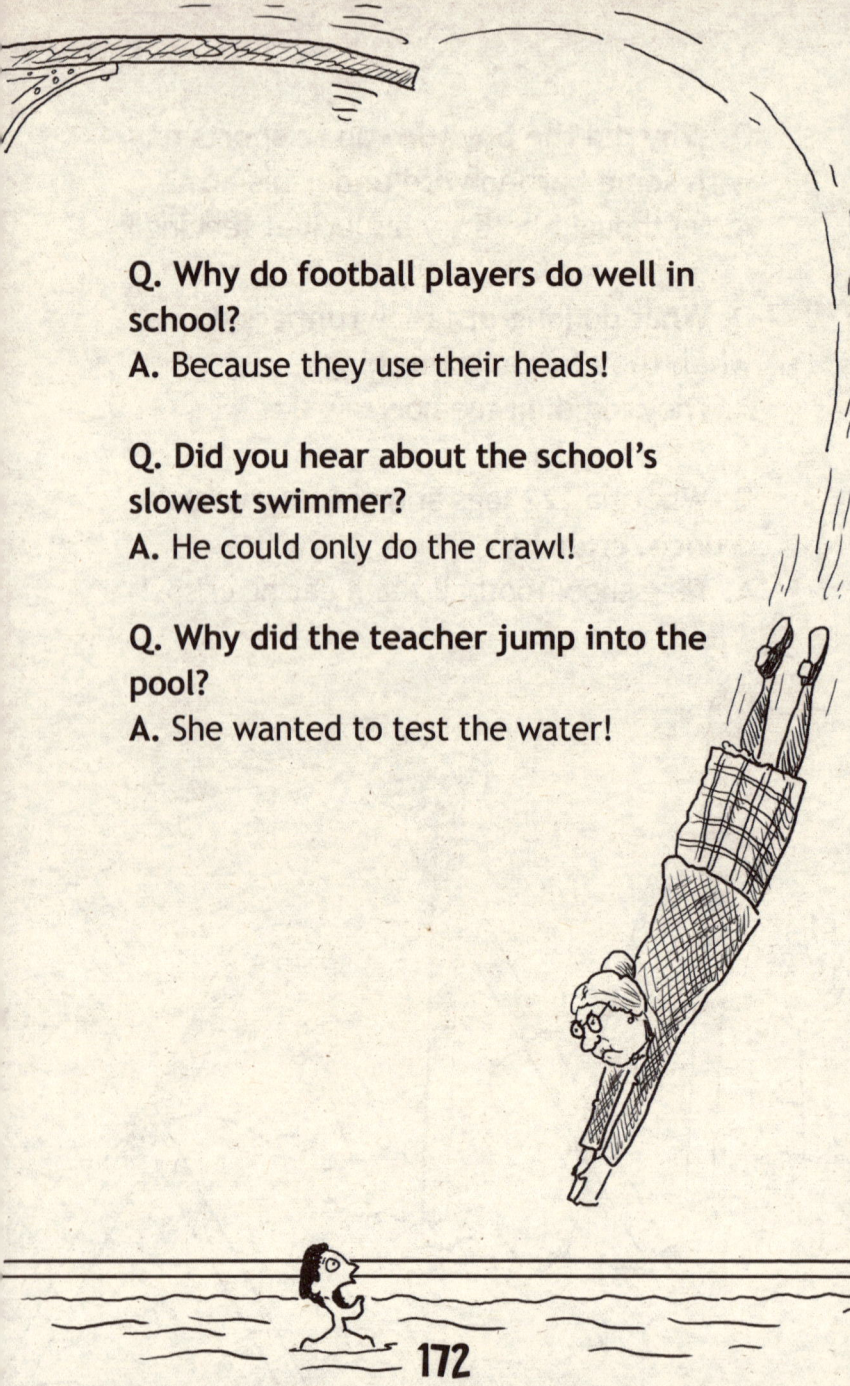

Q. Why do football players do well in school?
A. Because they use their heads!

Q. Did you hear about the school's slowest swimmer?
A. He could only do the crawl!

Q. Why did the teacher jump into the pool?
A. She wanted to test the water!

Tennis Tomfoolery

Q. What sport are waiters best at?
A. Tennis, because they can serve so well!

Q. What's tennis player's favourite city?
A. Volleywood!

Q. What can you serve but never eat?
A. A tennis ball!

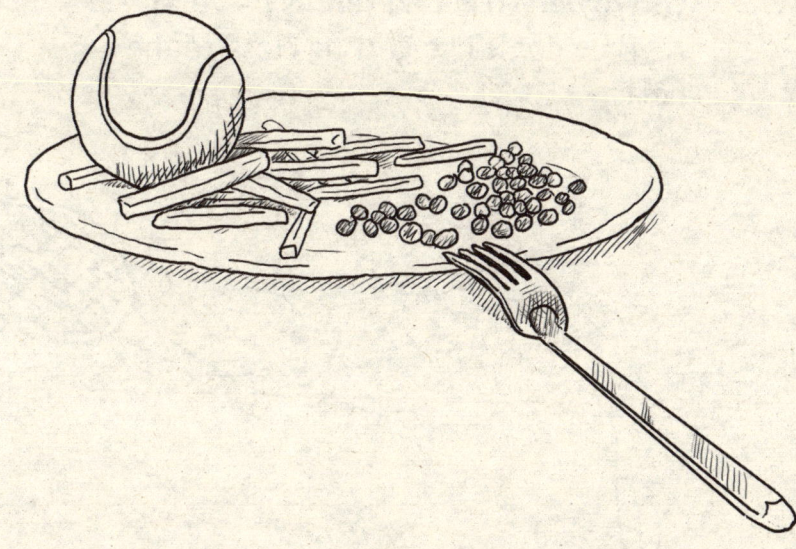

Knock, knock.
Who's there?
Tennis.
Tennis who?
Tennis five plus five!

Q. Why are tennis players bad at relationships?
A. Nobody wants to have love!

Q. Why did the tennis player hold his shoe to his ear?
A. Because he liked sole music!

Q. Why are fish bad tennis players?
A. They don't like getting close to the net!

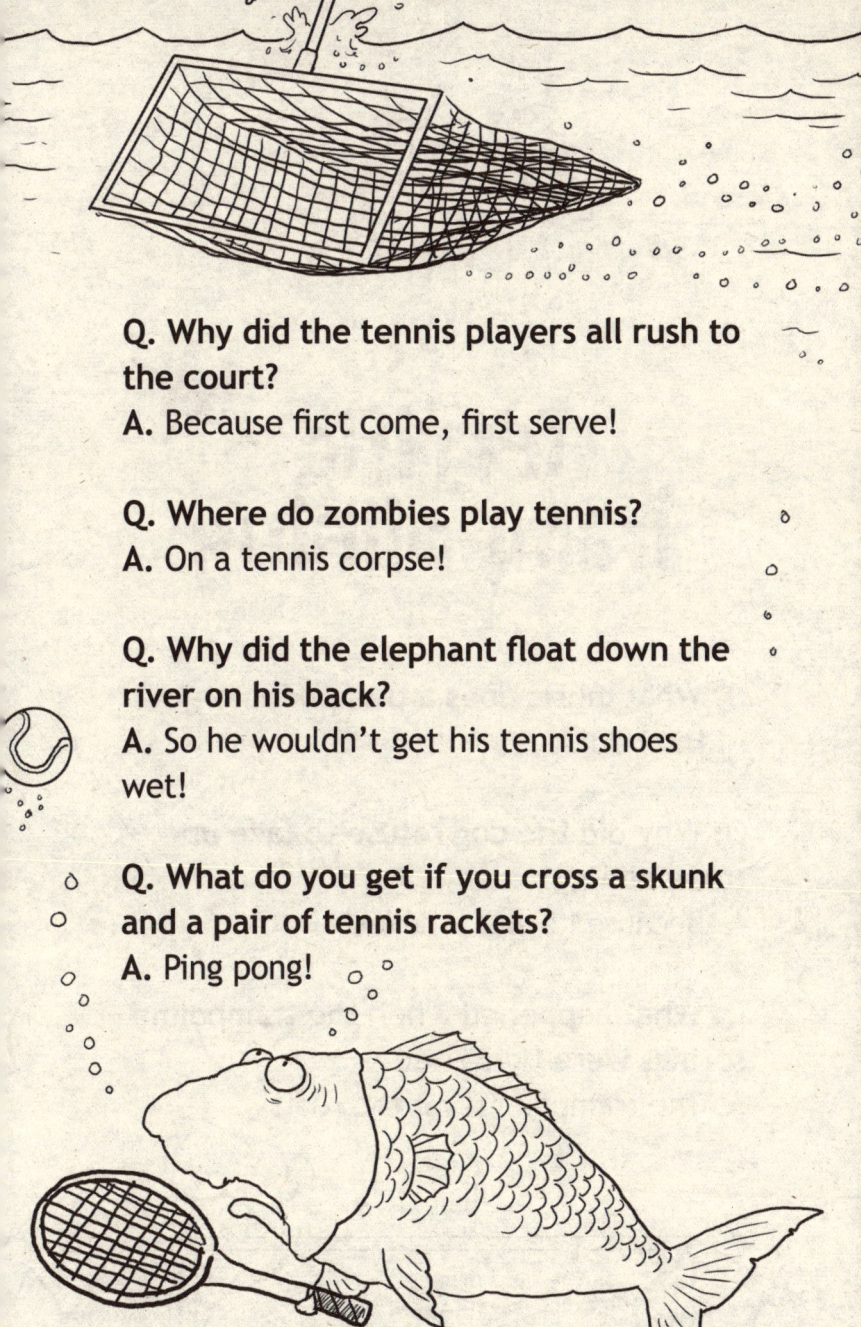

Q. Why did the tennis players all rush to the court?
A. Because first come, first serve!

Q. Where do zombies play tennis?
A. On a tennis corpse!

Q. Why did the elephant float down the river on his back?
A. So he wouldn't get his tennis shoes wet!

Q. What do you get if you cross a skunk and a pair of tennis rackets?
A. Ping pong!

terrific trampolining

Q. What music does a trampoline enjoy?
A. Hip Hop!

Q. Why did the dog refuse to take up trampolining?
A. Because he was a Boxer!

Q. What happened when the trampoline springs were tightened?
A. The trampolinist hit the roof!

Q. Why wasn't the trampolinist surprised when she won a gold medal?
A. She always knew she would reach great heights!

Q. Why do trampoline coaches enjoy their job?
A. Because of the ups and downs!

Q. What do trampolinists do when they get ill?
A. Hope they bounce back soon!

Q. What is the best time of year to take up trampolining?
A. Spring!

Wacky Weightlifting

Q. What bird is the best weightlifter?
A. The crane!

Q. Did you hear about the weightlifting vegetable?
A. He was a muscle sprout!

Q. Why did the weightlifter strap a dictionary to each arm?
A. He wanted his arms to have definition!

Q. What makes a weightlifter smile?
A. His facial muscles!

Witty Wrestling

Q. Why did the wrestler always carry a key?
A. To get out of hammerlocks!

Q. What do wrestler's drinks come in?
A. Six packs!

1st Wrestler: I hear you're taking a mail-order bodybuilding course?
2nd Wrestler: Yes. Every week, the postman brings me a new piece of bodybuilding equipment.
1st Wrestler: You don't look any different though.
2nd Wrestler: I know, but you should see how muscular my postman is!

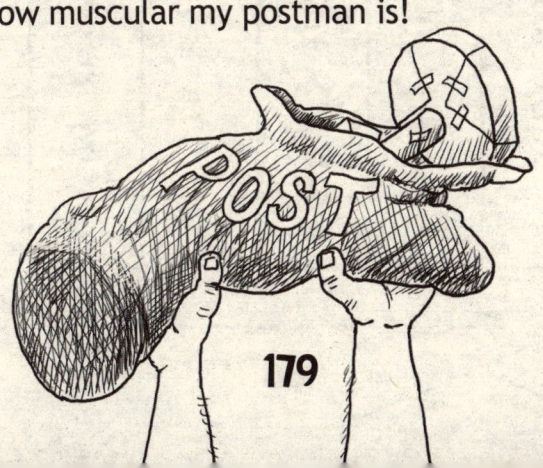

Smashing Sports Books

- 'RUNNING SLOWLY' BY ISA COMING
- 'Will He Win?' by Betty Wont
- 'Coping with Losing at Sports' by Anne Guish
- 'He Must Win' by Elsie Cries
- 'Knocked Out' by Esau Stars
- 'World's Greatest Wrestlers' by Everhard Muscles
- 'Kung Fu With Your Chums' by Flora Friend

- 'FEELING LIKE A WINNER' BY U. DUNNIT
- 'The Worst Striker' by Mr Goal
- 'PENALTY SHOOT-OUTS' BY HUGO FIRST
- 'My Greatest Goals' by Annette Buster
- 'How To Put Your Football Boots On' by Neil Down
- 'KEEP ON TRYING' BY PERCY VERE
- 'THE DAY AFTER A MARATHON' BY A. KING
- 'How I Win Races' by Aaron Quigley

- 'Golfer's Sandwich' by B. L. Tee
- 'ARCHERY FOR BEGINNERS' BY BEAU N. ARROW
- 'Shooting Arrows' by Anne Archer
- 'Rock Climbing for Beginners' by Andover Hand
- 'First Time in the Boxing Ring' by Emma Fraid
- 'World Champion Boxer' by Amanda B. Reckondwith
- 'Competitive Running' by Adam Muhway

School Jokes

Ready for School

Q. Why did the boy take a ladder to school?
A. Because it was a high school

Early one Monday morning, a mum walked into her son's room and said, "Up. Up. It's time to go to school."
The son replied, "I don't want to go to school."
"You have to go," the mum said.
"I hate that school. The kids are all mean and nasty."
"You still have to go," the mum insisted.
"It's like a jungle. One nasty fight after another. They threaten me at least 100 times a day!" cried the son.
"You have to go to school!"
"Why do I have to?" pleaded the son.
"Because," replied the mother, "You're the headmaster!"

Q. Why was the broom late for school?
A. He over swept.

Teacher: Do you know what time we start school here in the morning?
Pupil: No, Miss, I don't. I've never been here for that.

Teacher: Young man, how would you like it if I were ten minutes late for school every morning like you are?
Pupil: It would be great. We could walk to school together.

Teacher: What excuse have you got for being late?
Pupil: I ran so fast that I didn't have time to think of one.

Teacher: Why are you late?
Pupil: I'm not, Miss, my watch is set to American time, and I'm actually quite early!

Teacher: I think you rushed to school today. You have your shoes on the wrong feet.
Pupil: No I don't, Sir. These are the only feet I have.

Teacher: Do you have any idea how many times you've been late for school this year?
Pupil: Well, Miss, I don't think it's been more than once a day.

Q. What runs around the playground without moving?
A. The fence.

Q. Where do door-makers get their education?
A. The school of hard knocks.

Q. Why do magicians do so well in school?
A. They're good at trick questions.

Q. What type of school do surfers go to?
A. Boarding school.

Pupil: I'm sorry I'm late, Sir. I was having a dream about football.
Teacher: How did that make you late for school?
Pupil: They played extra time.

Teacher: You're late! You should have been here at nine o'clock.
Pupil: Why, Sir, what happened?

Our Quirky Head Teacher

Head teacher: Class, we will have only half a day of school this morning.
Pupils: Hooray!
Head teacher: We will have the other half this afternoon!
Pupils: Boo!

Parent: What did you do at school today?
Pupil: We did a guessing game.
Parent: But I thought you were having a maths exam?
Pupil: That's right!

Head teacher: I despair, how do you manage to get so many things wrong in one day?
Pupil: Because I always get here early, Sir!

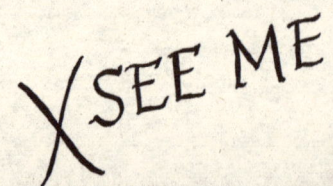

Q. Why did the clock go to the head teacher's office?
A. For tocking too much!

Head teacher: Young lady, why are you hopping on one leg?
Pupil: Well, Sir, you told me not to walk in late again.

Head teacher: Why do you have a sausage behind your ear?
Pupil: Oh no! I must have eaten my pencil for lunch.

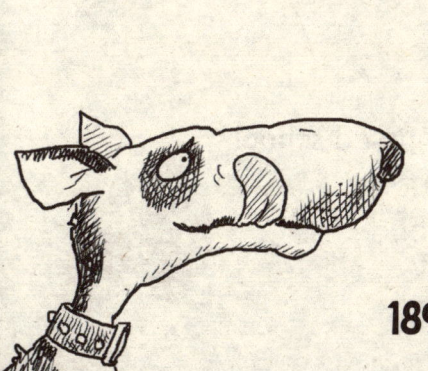

Head teacher: Why is your test score so low?
Pupil: It's because of sickness.
Head teacher: You were off sick?
Pupil: No, the girl next to me was.

Head teacher: Young man, your essay called '*My Dog*' is exactly the same as your brother's. Did you copy his?
Pupil: No, Sir. It's the same dog.

Head teacher: You missed school yesterday, didn't you?
Pupil: Not very much!

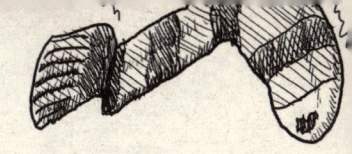

Q. Why did the head teacher take his pupils up in an aeroplane?
A. Because he wanted them to get higher grades.

Head teacher: Every time I turn around, I catch you doing something you're not supposed to be doing. What can we do about that?
Pupil: Tell me when you're going to turn around.

Head teacher: You're the number one troublemaker in this school.
Pupil: See? And my parents said I'd never amount to anything.

Q. Why couldn't the giraffe go to school?
A. Because it wasn't a HIGH school.

Head teacher: Name two days of the week that start with 't'.
Pupil: Today and Tomorrow.

Head teacher: Why weren't you in school yesterday?
Pupil: I was sick, Sir.
Head teacher: Sick of what?
Pupil: Sick of school.

Head teacher: Young man, I think when you grow up you should become a baker.
Pupil: Why is that, Sir?
Head teacher: Because all you have done at school is loaf around.

Head teacher: Why were you late?
Pupil: Sorry, Miss, I overslept.
Head teacher: You mean you sleep at home as well as at school?

Head teacher: Young lady, give me a sentence containing the word 'gruesome'.
Pupil: My dad didn't shave for a week and grew some whiskers.

Head teacher: Why are you standing on your head in the corridor?
Pupil: I'm just turning things over in my mind, Sir!

tee-hee-hee Teachers

Teacher: You aren't paying attention to me. Are you having trouble hearing?
Pupil: No, Sir, I'm having trouble listening!

Q. Why are reception teachers so good?
A. They can make little things count.

Q. Why do teachers tell you off for whispering?
A. Because it's not aloud.

Q. What is a maths teacher's favourite sum?
A. Summer!

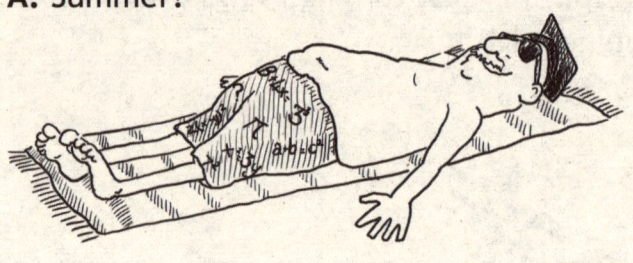

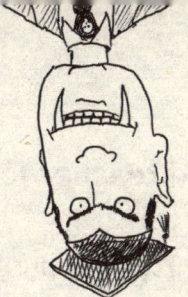

Q. What do you get when you cross a teacher and a vampire?
A. Lots of blood tests!

Q. Why did the teacher send Dracula home from school?
A. Because he disturbed the class with his constant coffin.

Q. Why did the teacher go to the beach?
A. To test the water.

Q. Why did the teacher marry the school caretaker?
A. Because he swept her off her feet!

Q. Why did the cross-eyed teacher lose her job?
A. Because she couldn't control her pupils.

Q. What do you call a teacher without students?
A. Happy.

Q. How do teachers get dressed in winter?
A. Quickly.

Q. Why did the teacher tie all her pupils' shoelaces together?
A. She wanted to go on a class trip!

Q. What are the two best things about being a teacher?
A. July and August.

Q. Why did the boy take a car to school?
A. He wanted to drive the teacher up the wall.

Q. Where do pupils learn to make banana splits?
A. At sundae school.

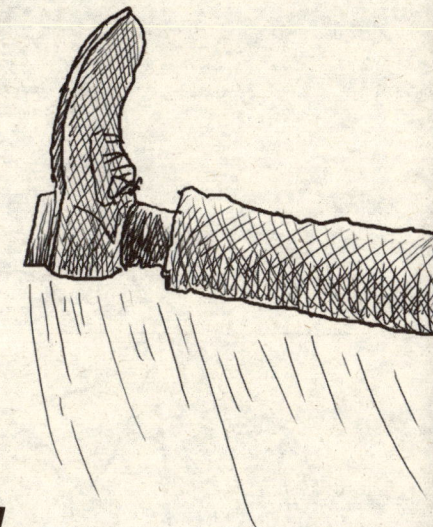

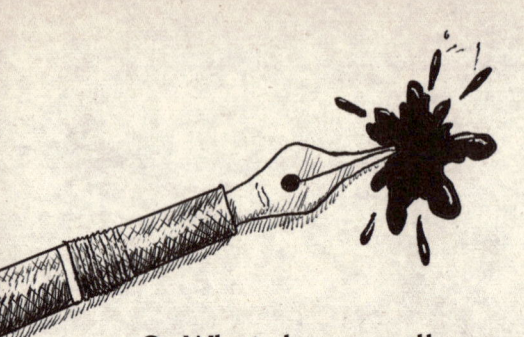

Q. What do you call someone who keeps talking when no one else is listening?
A. A teacher

Q. Why are teachers special?
A. They are in a class of their own.

Q. Why did the Cyclops give up teaching?
A. He only ever had one pupil.

Teacher: This note from your father looks like your handwriting?
Pupil: Well, yes, he borrowed my pen!

Teacher: I wished you would pay a little attention.
Pupil: I'm paying as little as I can!

Q. What tests do teachers set at witch school?
A. Hex-aminations!

Pupil: Sir, why aren't pencils made with erasers on both ends?
Teachers: They would be pointless.

English Class Capers

Q. Why was the school library evacuated?
A. Because someone found 'dynamite' in the dictionary.

Q. Where do pencils go on holiday?
A. Pencil-vania.

Q. What type of bus can't you ride?
A. A syllabus.

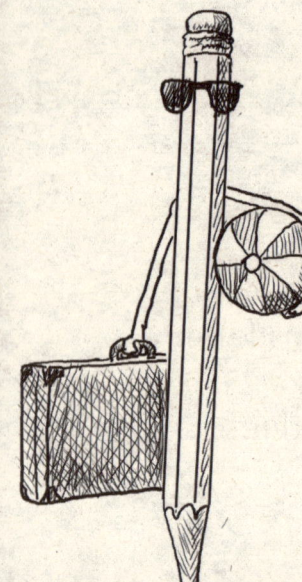

Teacher: Your poem is the worst in the class. It's not only badly spelled, it's rude and in bad taste. I'm going to send your father a note about it.
Pupil: I don't think that would help, Sir. He wrote it.

Q. Which play did Shakespeare write for baby pigs?
A. Hamlet.

Q. Why is an English teacher like a judge?
A. Because they both give out sentences.

Teacher: Simon, can you say your name backwards?
Simon: No Mis.

Teacher: Which word starts with e, ends with e and has a letter in it?
Pupil: Envelope

Q. When is a blue schoolbook not a blue schoolbook?
A. When it is read!

Teacher: Give me a sentence with the word centimetre in it.
Pupil: My auntie came to stay and I was sent ta meet 'er.

X SEE ME

TEST

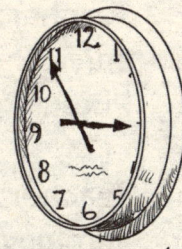

Teacher: Can you give me an example of a double negative?
Pupil: I don't know none.
Teacher: Excellent!

Teacher: Can you name two pronouns?
Pupil: Who, me?
Teacher: Correct!

Q. Which 7 letters might you say when you open the fridge and find nothing inside?
A. O I C U R M T

Teacher: What did you write your essay on?
Pupil: A piece of paper.

Teacher: What is an autobiography?
Pupil: A car's life story.

Teacher: Why should we never use the word 'ain't?'
Pupil: Because it ain't correct.

Q. What insect can be spelled with just one letter?
A. Bee.

Teacher: What is the plural of mouse?
Pupil: Mice
Teacher: Good, now what's the plural of baby?
Pupil: Twins!

Teacher: What's the longest word in the English language?
Pupil: Smiles – because there is a mile between the first and last letters!

Teacher: Why are you wearing a collar around your neck?
Pupil: Because I want to be the teacher's pet!

Q. What is at the end of everything?
A. The letter G.

Q. Why do witches find English class so easy?
A. Because they are naturally good at spell-ings.

Q. Why does it take pirates so long to learn the alphabet?
A. Because they often get stuck at C!

Q. What goes on and on and has an 'i' in the middle?
A. An onion

on-1-on

Teacher: I want you to tell me the longest sentence you can think of.
Pupil: Life imprisonment!

Knock, knock.
Who's there?
Needle.
Needle who?
Needle little help making this poem rhyme!

Side-Splitting Science Lab

Q. If H_2O is the formula for water, what is the formula for ice?
A. H_2O cubed.

Q. What is the centre of gravity?
A. The letter V.

Q. What smells most in the science lab?
A. Your nose.

Q. If we breathe oxygen during the day, what do we breathe at night?
A. Nitrogen.

Q. Why did the cell cross the microscope?
A. To get to the other slide.

Teacher: Can you tell me why the law of gravity is useful?
Pupil: If we drop something, it's much easier to get it off the floor than off the ceiling.

Q. What is the happiest thing in the sky?
A. The sun. It's always beaming.

TEST

Teacher: Name a conductor of electricity.
Pupil: Why... er...
Teacher: Wire is right. Name a unit of electrical power.
Pupil: What?
Teacher: The watt is absolutely correct.

Q. What happens if you swallow uranium?
A. You get an atomic ache.

Teacher: Can you name a blue-white metal?
Pupil: Let me zinc about it.

Q. What do you call the leader of a biology gang?
A. The Nucleus.

Q. What is the difference between an African elephant and an Indian elephant?
A. About 3,000 miles.

Q. Why do bees have sticky hair?
A. Because they have honeycombs.

Q. What would you get if you crossed vegetables with a necklace?
A. A food chain.

Q. What kind of ghosts haunt the school chemistry labs?
A. Methylated spirits.

Q. Why is electricity so dangerous?
A. Because it doesn't know how to conduct itself properly.

Teacher: Can you name four members of the cat family?
Pupil: Daddy cat, mummy cat and two kittens!

Q. What is the difference between a dog and a marine biologist?
A. One wags a tail and the other tags a whale.

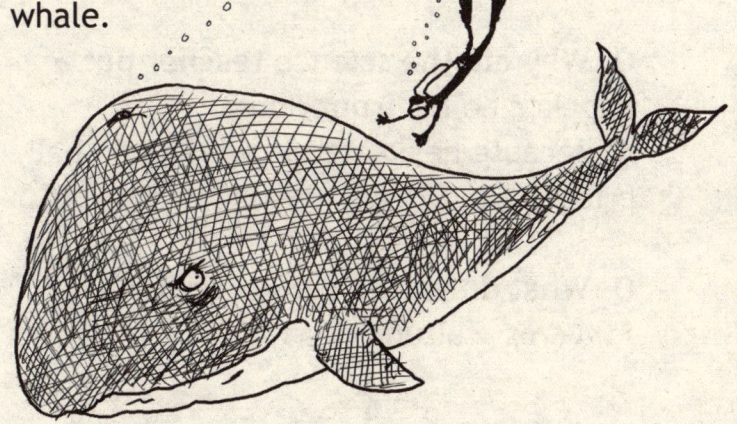

Q. What did the femur say to the patella?
A. I kneed you.

Q. How do you identify a bald eagle?
A. All his feathers are combed over to one side.

Q. How do science teachers freshen their breath?
A. With experi-mints.

Q. Why did the science teacher put a knocker on his front door?
A. Because he wanted to win the no-bell prize.

Q. What do you call angry bacteria?
A. A cross culture.

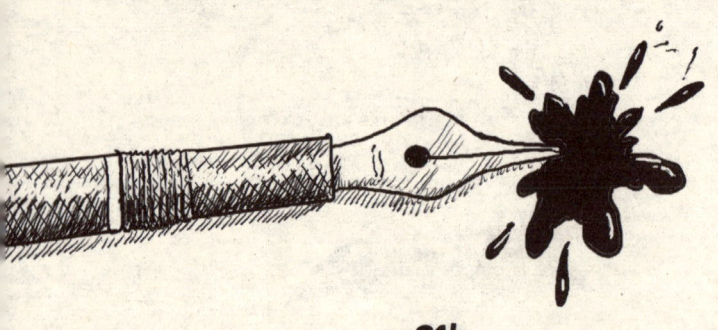

Rowdy Music Lesson

Q. Why do music teachers always buy expensive violins?
A. Because cheap ones might be a fiddle.

Q. What musical instruments do pirates play?
A. The loot.

Q. Which musical instrument is good for fishermen?
A. The castanet.

Q. Why do music teachers call pianos noble instruments?
A. Because most are upright, but some are grand.

Q. Which musical instruments do you have in your body?
A. Your eardrums.

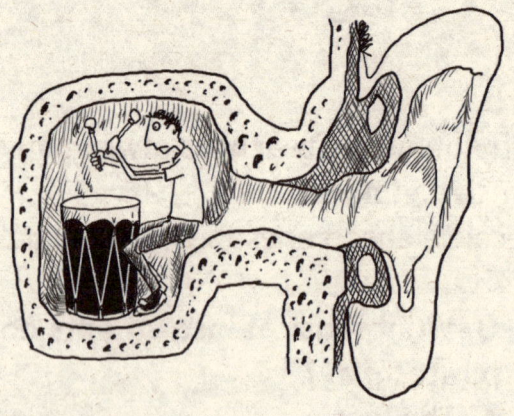

Q. Why did the pupils get into trouble in music class?
A. They were passing notes.

Q. Why was the music teacher arrested?
A. She got into treble.

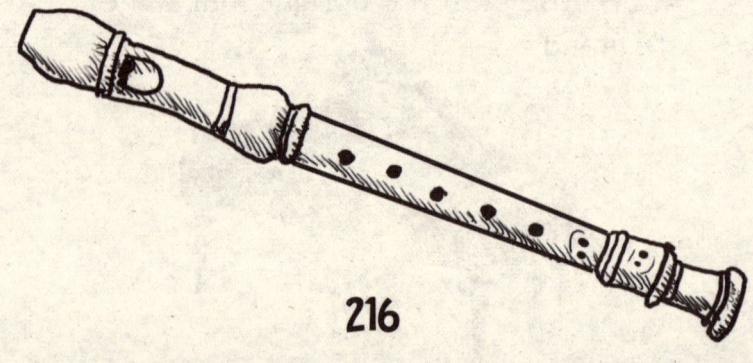

Q. Where does the music teacher write her music?
A. In a notebook.

Q. What do music teachers have on their beds?
A. Sheet music.

Q. Why did the music teacher go up the ladder during music class?
A. To reach the high notes!

Q. Why did the music teacher keep a goldfish in his classroom?
A. So he could remember his scales.

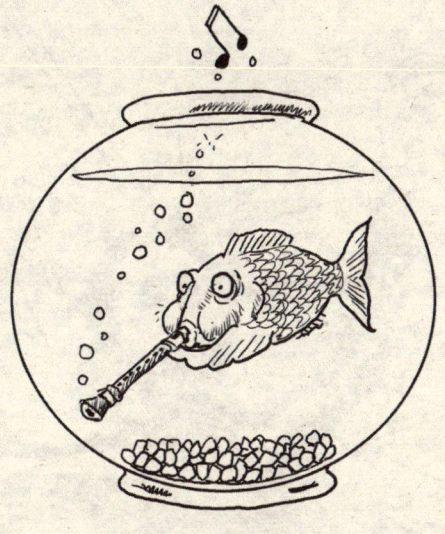

Q. What kind of band can't play music?
A. A rubber band.

Q. What makes music on your hair?
A. A headband!

Q. Who got hit by lightning when the school orchestra played in a storm?
A. The conductor.

Q. What type of music are balloons scared of?
A. Pop music!

Q. What's the difference between a piano and a fish?
A. You can tune a piano, but you can't tuna fish!

Q. Why was the music teacher angry with the school athletics team?
A. Because they broke a record!

Q. What has forty feet and sings?
A. The school choir!

Q. What's the difference between a jet aeroplane and a trumpet?
A. About three decibels.

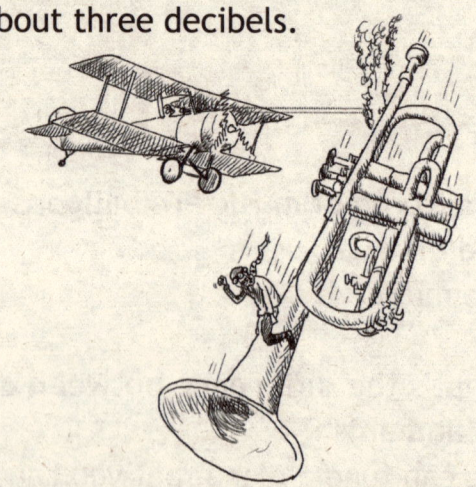

Q. Why couldn't the music teacher open her classroom?
A. Because her keys were on the piano.

Q. What did a music teacher say to a tightrope walker?
A. You better C sharp or you'll B flat!

Q. Did you hear about the music teacher who kept banging his head against the keys?
A. He was playing by ear.

Q. What type of songs do the planets sing?
A. Nep-tunes!

Q. Why do fluorescent lights hum?
A. Because they forgot the words.

Knock knock!
Who's there?
Little old lady?
Little old lady who?
Wow! I didn't know you could yodel!

School Lunchtimes LOLs

Q. What did the egg say to the frying pan?
A. You crack me up!

Q. How do you know when they are serving salad in the school canteen?
A. When you can't smell anything burning.

Q. What is the school cook's motto?
A. If at first you don't succeed, fry, fry and fry again.

Q. What nut sounds like a sneeze?
A. A cashew.

Q. What swings through French school dining rooms?
A. The lunch pack of Notre Dame.

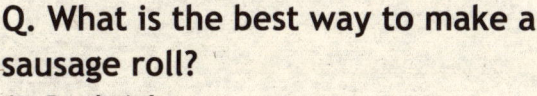

Q. What is the best way to make a sausage roll?
A. Push it!

Q. What's the difference between a hungry pupil and a greedy pupil?
A. A hungry pupil longs to eat, while a greedy pupil eats too long.

Q. What is the worst thing you will find in the school canteen?
A. The food!

Q. Why do the eggs taste funny in the school canteen?
A. Because they are always playing practical yokes.

Q. What did the school cook do to celebrate his engagement?
A. He gave his girlfriend an onion ring.

Q. How do you kill someone with a school lunch?
A. Eggsterminate them.

Q. Why was the school cook cruel?
A. Because she batters fish, beats eggs and whips cream.

Q. Why did the boy stare at his carton of juice?
A. Because it said concentrate.

Pupil: Miss, there is a bar of soap in my soup!
Dinner lady: That's to wash it down.

Q. Where did the spaghetti go to dance?
A. The meat ball.

Pupil: Miss, this egg is disgusting!
Dinner lady: Don't blame me, I only laid the table.

Pupil: Miss, this egg soup tastes funny!
Dinner lady: So, why aren't you laughing?

Dinner lady: How did you find the steak today?
Pupil: I just moved a potato and there it was!

Pupil: Miss, should I eat this chicken with my fingers?
Dinner lady: No, the fingers should be eaten separately.

Pupil: Miss, why is there a button in my salad?
Dinner lady: It must have fallen off when the salad was dressing.

Q. What table can you eat?
A. A vege-table

Dinner lady: Eat your greens, they are good for your skin.
Pupil: But I don't want green skin!

Q. Why does the Religious Studies teacher love Swiss cheese?
A. Because it's hole-y

Hilarious History Class

Q. What do history teachers talk about in the staff room?
A. The good old days.

Q. Which historical figure invented fractions?
A. Henry the ⅛th!

Q. What's purple and 5,000 miles long?
A. The grape wall of China.

Q. Where was the Magna Carta signed?
A. At the bottom.

Q. What was carved into the door of the pharaoh's tomb?
A. Toot 'n' come in.

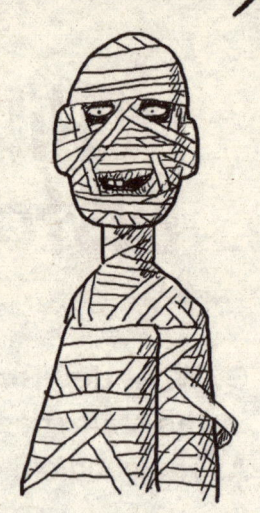

Q. When were the Middle Ages?
A. Between the first and the last ones.

Q. What happened after the wheel was invented?
A. There was a revolution.

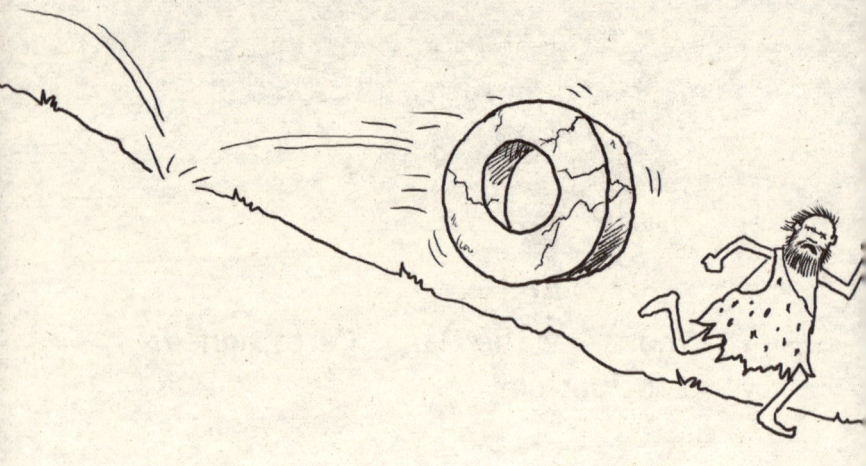

Q. Where would you find a prehistoric cow?
A. At a moo-seum.

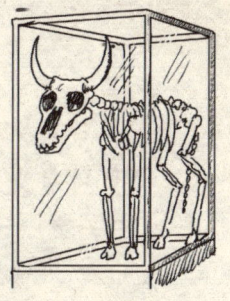

Q. Was Rome built in a day?
A. No, it was built in Italy.

Q. Where are the kings and queens of England usually crowned?
A. On their heads.

Q. Why was school easier for cave people?
A. Because there was no history to study!

Teacher: What came after the Stone Age and the Bronze Age?
Pupil: The saus-age!

Q. What was Camelot famous for?
A. Its knight life!

Teacher: Can you describe Camelot?
Pupil: Is that the place where people parked their camels?

Q. Why did King Arthur have a round table?
A. So no one could corner him!

Q. Who invented King Arthur's round table?
A. Sir Circumference!

Q. What was King Arthur's favourite game?
A. Knights and crosses!

Q. When were King Arthur's army too tired to fight?
A. When they had lots of sleepless knights!

Teacher: Why does history keep repeating itself?
Pupils: Because we weren't listening the first time!

Q. Where do soldiers keep their armies?
A. Up their sleevies!

Q. Why did the Romans build straight roads?
A. So their soldiers didn't go round the bend!

Q. What do Alexander the Great and Kermit the Frog have in common?
A. The same middle name!

Q. What is the fruitiest subject at school?
A. History, because it's full of dates!

Q. How was the Roman Empire cut in half?
A. With a pair of Caesars!

Q. When a knight in armour was killed in battle, what sign did they put on his grave?
A. Rust in peace!

Q. How did the Vikings send secret messages?
A. By Norse code!

Teacher: What is a forum?
Pupil: Is it two-um plus two-um?

Q. Why did Henry VIII have so many wives?
A. He liked to chop and change!

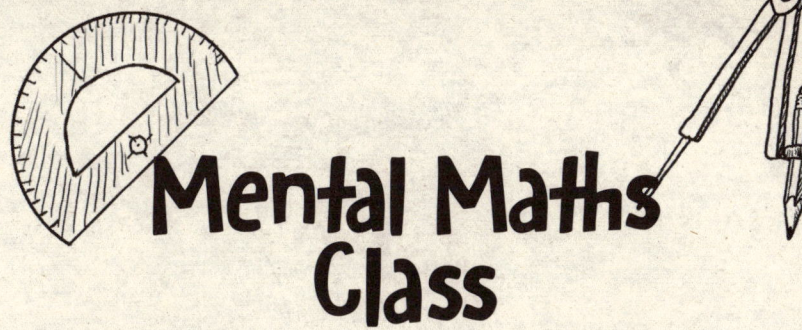

Mental Maths Class

Q. What's the longest piece of furniture in school?
A. The multiplication table.

Q. What kind of food do maths teachers love?
A. Square meals.

Q. What is a maths teacher's favourite food?
A. Pi!

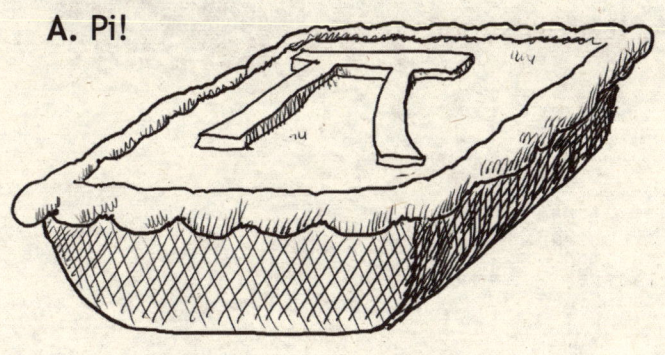

Q. Why was the maths book sad?
A. Because it had too many problems.

Q. What happened to the plant in maths class?
A. It grew square roots.

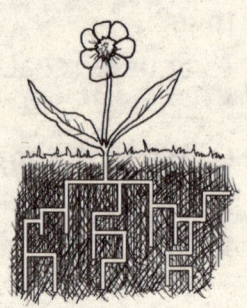

Q. What did the number 0 say to number 8?
A. Nice belt!

Q. What type of tree did the maths teacher climb?
A. A geometry.

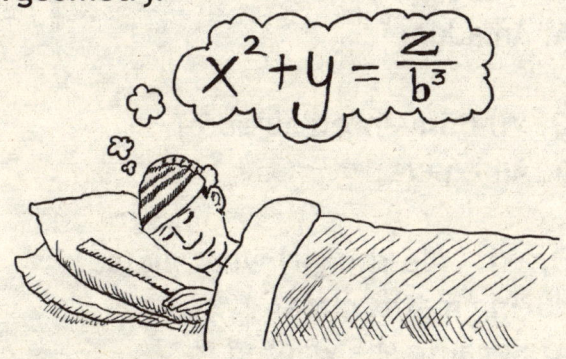

Q. Why did the maths teacher take a ruler to bed?
A. He wanted to see how long he slept.

Q. What is a polygon?
A. A dead parrot.

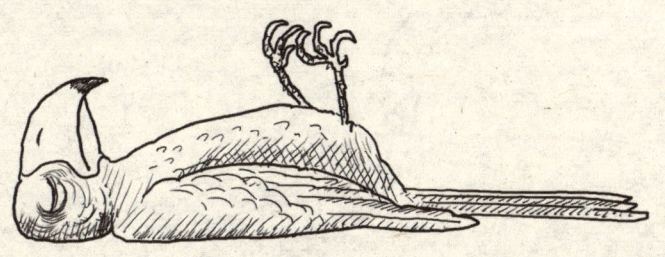

Q. Why didn't the two number 4's feel like having dinner?
A. Because they already 8.

Q. Which reptile is good at maths?
A. An adder.

Q. Who invented algebra?
A. An X-pert

Q. Why did the girl wear glasses during maths class?
A. Because she wanted to understand de-vision!

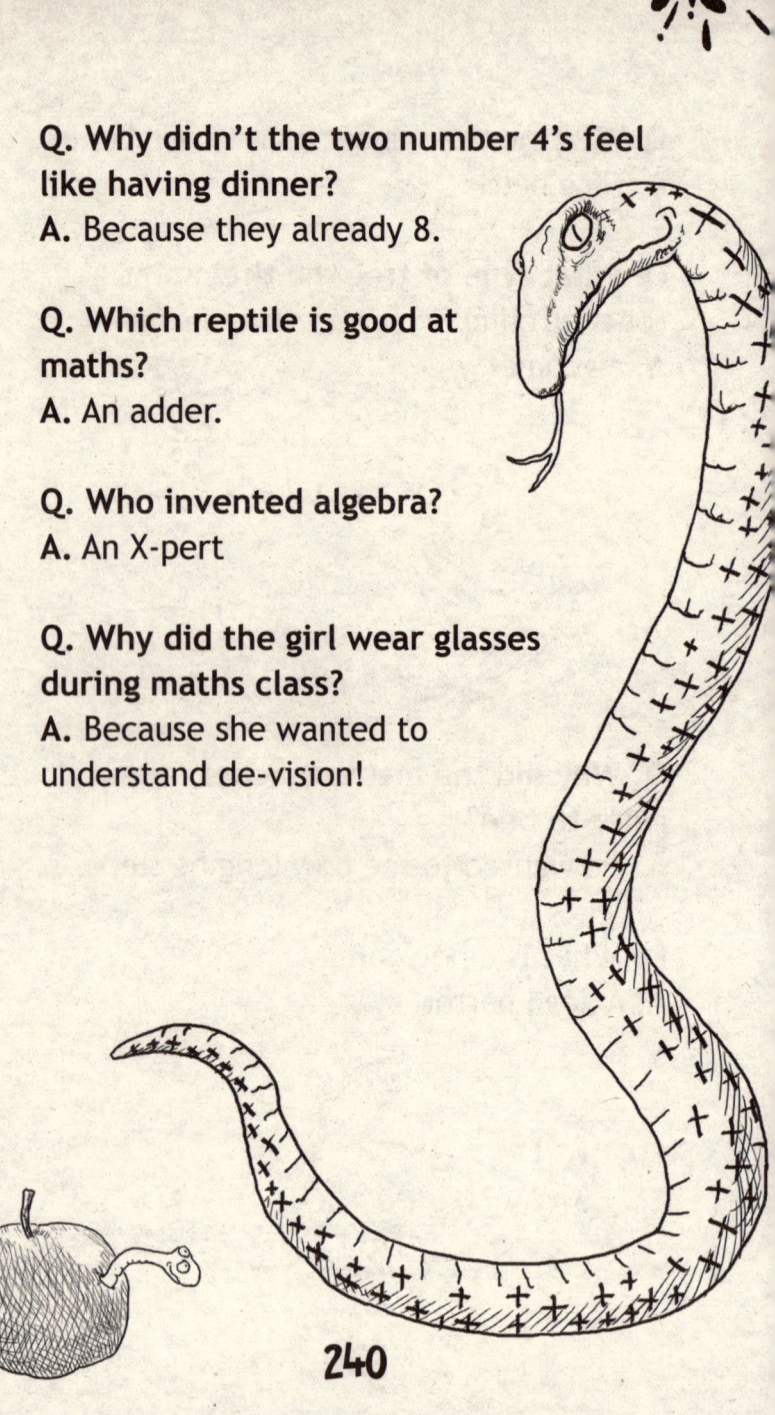

Q. What tool should you always take to maths class?
A. Multipliers.

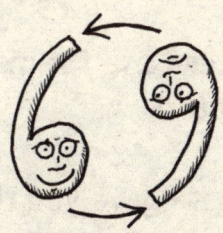

Q. What is bigger when it is upside down?
A. The number 6.

Q. What did one calculator say to the other?
A. You can count on me!

Q. What do you call friends who love maths?
A. Algebros

Q. What do ducks use for maths?
A. A QUACK-ulator!

Teacher: Now, if I gave you three rabbits, then the next day I gave you five rabbits, how many would you have?
Pupil: Nine, Sir.
Teacher: Nine?
Pupil: Yes, Sir. I've got one already!

Teacher: If you have £20 and I ask you for £10 as a loan, how many pounds would you still have?
Pupil: Twenty.
Teacher: What do you mean?
Pupil: Just because you ask me to loan you £10, it doesn't mean I am going to.

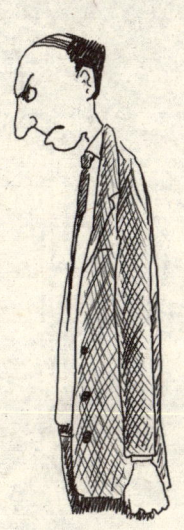

Teacher: How much is half of 8?
Pupil: Up and down, or across?
Teacher: What do you mean?
Pupil: Well, up and down makes a 3 and across the middle makes a 0!

Q. Where do you find a dead maths teacher?
A. Asymmetry

Q. How do you make seven an even number?
A. Take the 's' out!

Q. Why can't you do a maths test in the jungle?
A. There are too many cheetahs!

Q. If there are ten cats in a boat and one jumps out, how many are left?
A. None, they were all copycats!

Q. How many sides does a circle have?
A. Two, inside and out.

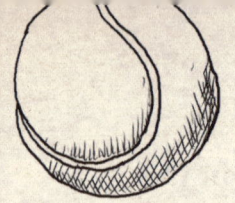

Silly Sports Class

Q. Which is the noisiest sport at school?
A. Tennis – because every player raises a racket.

Q. What happened when the two large schoolboys had a race?
A. One ran in short bursts and the other ran in burst shorts.

Q. What is harder to catch the faster you run?
A. Your breath.

Q. Why do you never see chickens playing football?
A. They are always getting sent off for fowl play.

Q. What is a frog's favourite sport?
A. Croak-et!

Q. What do you call a girl who stands between the goalposts?
A. Annette.

Q. Why did the cricket team ask the school cook to play?
A. They needed a good batter.

Q. What has eleven heads and runs around screaming?
A. A school hockey team.

Q. Why was Cinderella useless at all sports?
A. She had a pumpkin for a coach.

Q. Why was Cinderella thrown off the school football team?
A. She kept running away from the ball.

Q. Why is the school football pitch always wet?
A. Because the players dribble.

PE teacher: You never come first in anything.
Pupil: I'm always first in the dinner queue, Sir.

Q. Who was the fastest runner of all time?
A. Adam. He was first in the human race.

Q. Why did the school's best athlete lose the decathlon?
A. He had a slipped discus.

Q. What is the noisiest sport at school?
A. Racquetball.

Q. Why couldn't the shy boy go rock climbing?
A. He needed to be a little boulder.

Q. Which school athlete is the best looking?
A. The sprinter, because he's always dashing.

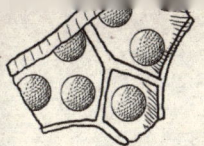

Q. Why should you wear two pairs of pants when playing golf?
A. Just in case you get a hole in one!

Q. Why did the PE teacher give the cricket team lighters?
A. Because they kept losing their matches.

Q. What is an insect's favourite sport?
A. Cricket

Q. When is a cricket game like a crime?
A. When there's a hit and run.

Q. What does the winner of a race lose?
A. His breath.

Q. Which class at school do runners like best?
A. Jog-raphy

Q. What position does the school ghost play in football?
A. Ghoulie!

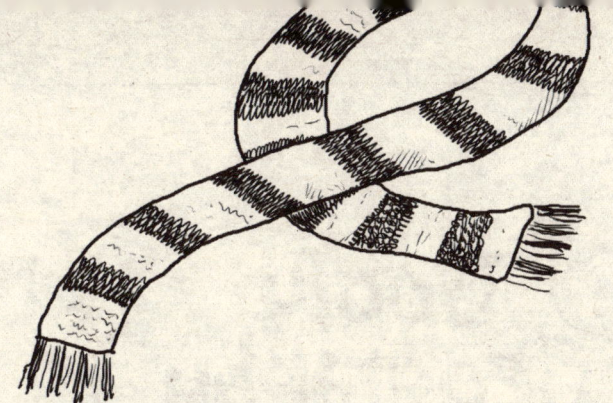

Q. Which athlete is the warmest in winter?
A. The long jumper.

Q. What can you serve but not eat?
A. A tennis ball.

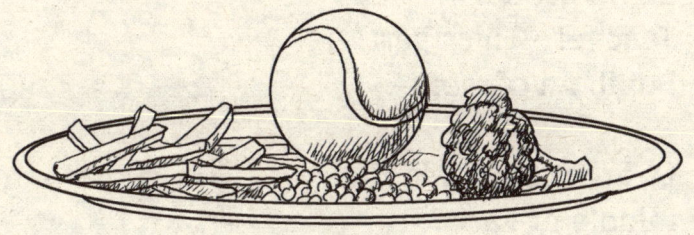

Goofy Geography

Q. What's 56 metres tall and is made out of pepperoni and cheese?
A. The leaning tower of Pizza.

Teacher: Where are you from young lady?
Pupil: Scotland.
Teacher: Which part?
Pupil: All of me.

Q. What stands in the middle of Paris?
A. The letter 'r'.

Q. What is a fjord?
A. A Swedish car.

Q. What has a bed that you can't sleep in?
A. A river.

Q. What are the small rivers that run into the Nile?
A. The juve-niles.

Q. What's the worst thing that can happen to a geography teacher?
A. Getting lost.

Q. How do mountains hear?
A. With mountain-ears.

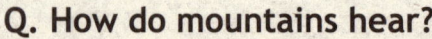

Q. What is the most shocking city in the world?
A. Electri-city.

Q. Where in France do all the houses have two bathrooms?
A. Toulouse.

Q. What did the ground say to the earthquake?
A. You crack me up!

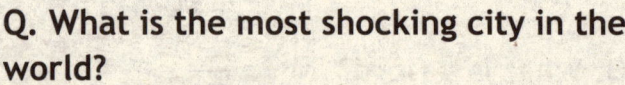

Q. What did the river say when the elephant sat in it?
A. Well I'll be dammed!

Q. What did the sea say to the shore?
A. Nothing, it just waved.

Teacher: Give me three reasons why the world is round.
Pupil: Well my dad says so, my mum says so and you say so!

Teacher: Can you name an animal that lives in Lapland?
Pupil: A reindeer.
Teacher: Good, now can you name another?
Pupil: Another reindeer!

Teacher: What's the coldest city in Germany?
Pupil: Brrrlin.

Teacher: Can you tell me where the Dead Sea is?
Pupil: I didn't even know it was sick.

Teacher: Do you think you may like to visit Egypt?
Pupil: Oh yes, I sphinx so.

Teacher: It's obvious that you haven't studied your geography. What's your excuse?
Pupil: Well, my dad says the world is changing every day. So, I decided to wait until it settles down.

Teacher: What is the definition of a volcano?
Pupil: A mountain that blows its top!

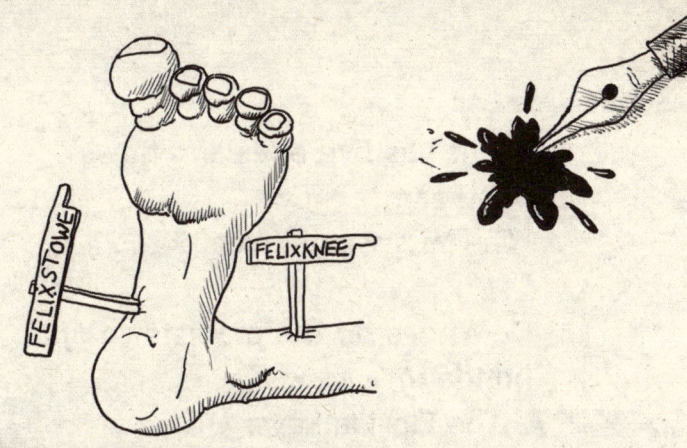

Teacher: Where is Felixstowe?
Pupil: At the end of his foot.

Teacher: Which is further away, Australia or the moon?
Pupil: Australia, you can see the moon at night!

Q. What has five eyes and flows downstream?
A. The Mississippi River.

Q. Where do the pianists go on holiday?
A. The Florida Keys.

Q. What stays in the corner, but travels around the world?
A. A stamp!

Q. What is the fastest country in the world?
A. Rush-a!

Art Class Antics

Q. Why did the art teacher take a pencil to bed?
A. So she could draw the curtains.

Q. What did the pencil say to the rubber?
A. Take me to your ruler.

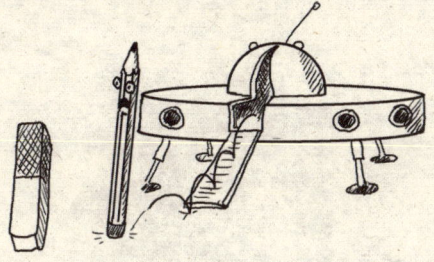

Q. Why did the student bring scissors to the art room?
A. He wanted to cut class!

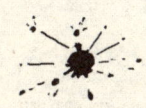

Q. What is a pirate's favourite subject?
A. Arrrrrrt!

Q. Why was the art teacher afraid he might go to jail?
A. Because he'd been framed!

Q. What happened when two art teachers had a race?
A. They drew.

Q. Why did the art teacher draw on the window?
A. To make the lesson very clear.

Q. What do you call an American style of drawing?
A. A yankee doodle.

Q. Why was the art dealer in debt?
A. He didn't have any Monet.

Teacher: I said to draw a cow eating some grass but you've only drawn the cow.
Pupil: Yes, the cow ate all the grass!

Q. What do you call an artist with a tickly throat?
A. Van Cough

Q. Why did the art teacher want to paint everything around her?
A. She was easelly inspired.

Q. Why was Dracula asked to leave the art class?
A. Because he could only draw blood.

Q. Why did the art teacher give up making pictures from broken bottles?
A. It's not really all that it's cracked up to be.

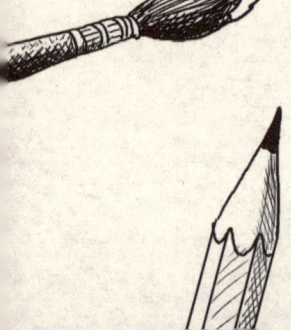

Q. What did the art teacher say to the dentist?
A. Matisse hurt.

Art teacher: I told the class to draw a horse and cart, but you have only drawn a horse!
Pupil: Yes, Sir, the horse will draw the cart!

Laughable Library

Q. Why didn't the thief burgle the library?
A. Because he was afraid the judge would give him a long sentence.

Q. Why did the librarian slip and fall in the library?
A. Because she strayed into the non-friction section.

Q. What did one book say to the other one?
A. I just want to see if we are on the same page.

Q. What do you do if your pet starts eating your library book?
A. Take the words right out of their mouth.

Q. Why are school librarians so lonely?
A. They are always by them shelves.

Pupil: Do you have any books on coincidences?
Librarian: As a matter of fact, this one's just arrived.

Q. Why don't most pupils know where the school library is?
A. They kept it quiet.

Laughable Library Books

Please Teach Me! by I. Wanda Know

April Fool! by Sue Prize

Come On In! by Doris Open

PARACHUTING FOR BEGINNERS BY HUGO FIRST

HOW TO GET RICH by Xavier Money

I Love Crowds by Morris Merrier

I Hit the Wall by Isadora There

I Didn't Do It! By Ivan Alibi

Wind Instruments by Tom Bone

Crocodile Dundee by Ali Gator

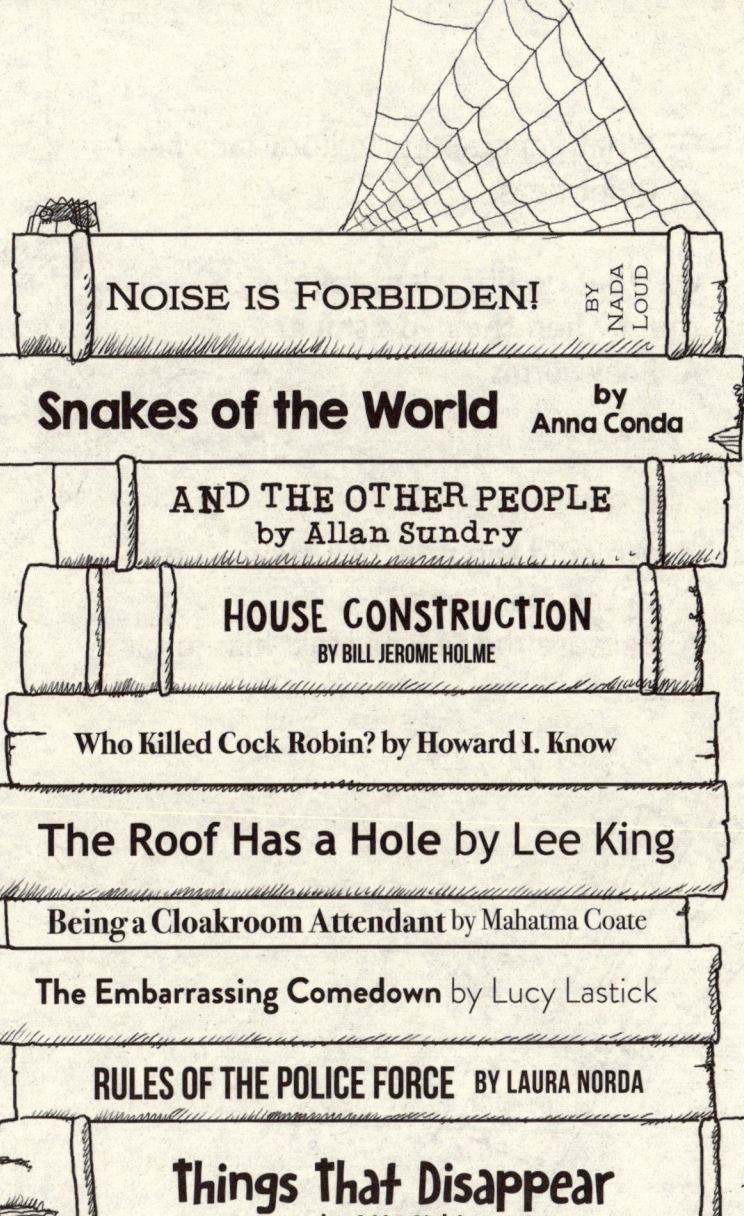

Q. What vegetables do librarians like?
A. Quiet peas.

Q. What do librarians take with them when they go fishing?
A. Bookworms.

Q. Why did the new boy steal a chair from the classroom?
A. Because the teacher told him to take a seat.

Hopeless Homework

Teacher: Why didn't you do your history homework?
Pupil: I didn't want to dwell on the past.

**Knock-Knock
Who's there?
Howl
Howl who?
Howl we ever finish our homework if we keep telling jokes?**

Teacher: Did you father help you with your homework?
Pupil: No, he did it all by himself.

Q. Why didn't the swamp creature go to the party?
A. He was bogged down with homework.

Q. Why did the boy eat his homework?
A. Because his teacher said it was a piece of cake.

Q. Why didn't the pirate do his homework?
A. It was too harrrrrd!

Knock, knock.
Who's there?
Canoe.
Canoe, who?
Canoe help me with my homework?

Teacher: Why haven't you done your maths homework?
Pupil: I have a solar powered calculator and it was cloudy last night

Pupil: I didn't do my homework because I lost my memory.
Teacher: When did this start?
Pupil: When did what start?

Q. What do elves do after school?
A. Their gnomework.

Pupil: Sir, I've been given too much homework, I can't do it all.
Teacher: Young man, hard work never killed anyone.
Pupil: I know, but I don't want to be the first.

Teacher: Johnny, what is the definition of 'infinity?'
Pupil: Tonight's homework by the look of it.

Teacher: Where is your homework?
Pupil: It blew away while I was walking to school.
Teacher: OK, but why are you late for school?
Pupil: I had to wait until it was really windy.

Teacher: How do you like doing your homework?
Pupil: I like doing nothing better.

**Knock, knock.
Who's there?
Gladys.
Gladys, who?
Gladys the weekend - no homework!**

Teacher: Where is your homework, young lady?
Pupil: My dog ate it?
Teacher: Honestly, do you really expect me to believe that?
Pupil: It's true! Once I had wrapped it up in ham, he chomped it down!

Disgusting Jokes

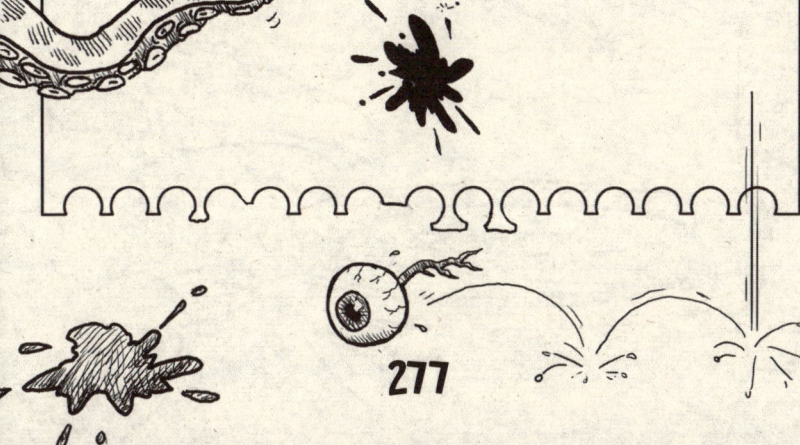

toilet tomfoolery

Q. Why did the toilet roll throw itself off the cliff?
A. Because it wanted to get to the bottom!

Q. What's brown, stinky and sounds like a bell?
A. Dung!

Q. What do you call a dog in your toilet?
A. A poodle!

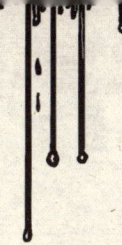

Q. What vegetable grows in a toilet?
A. A leek!

Q. When does 'q' come before 'p'?
A. At the public toilet!

Q. What did one toilet say to another?
A. You look a little flushed!

Q. Why do English teachers spend so long in the toilet?
A. They are always writing poo-ems!

Q. What do you call a woman with two toilets on her head?
A. Lulu!

Q. Did you hear the joke about the toilet?
A. Never mind, it's too dirty!

Q. What day of the week do most people get diarrhoea?
A. Splatter-day!

Q. Why did the beach smell bad?
A. Because the sea weed!

Q. What's the best way to keep flies out of your kitchen?
A. Keep a bucket of manure in the hallway!

Q. Have you heard about the new book *Constipation*?
A. It hasn't come out yet!

Q. Why did the nerd take toilet paper to the celebration?
A. Because he was a party pooper!

Q. Why did the child tell the toilet a joke?
A. Because she thought it looked down in the dumps!

Knock, knock.
Who's there?
Europe.
Europe who?
No you are!

Q. What's the only poo that doesn't smell bad?
A. Shampoo!

Q. What happens if you brush your teeth with chicken poo?
A. You get fowl breath!

Q. What's brown and sticky?
A. A stick!

Q. What do you call perfume made from diarrhoea?
A. Eau de Colon!

Q. What type of tree can't you climb?
A. A lavatory!

Q. What did William Shakespeare think when he sat on the toilet?
A. To pee or not to pee ... that is the question!

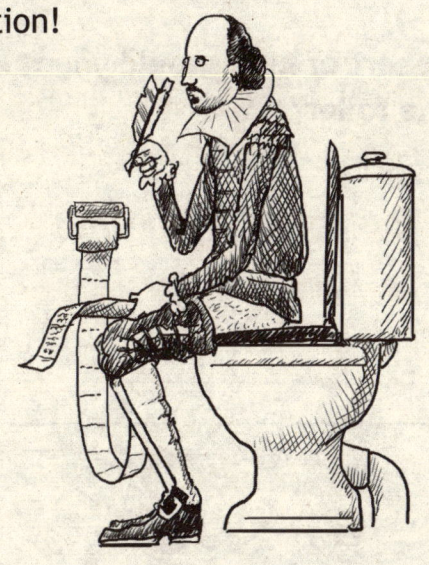

Q. Why was the footballer banned from using the bathroom?
A. He was always dribbling on the seat!

Q. Which swashbuckling heroes liked to urinate on their enemies?
A. The wee-musketeers!

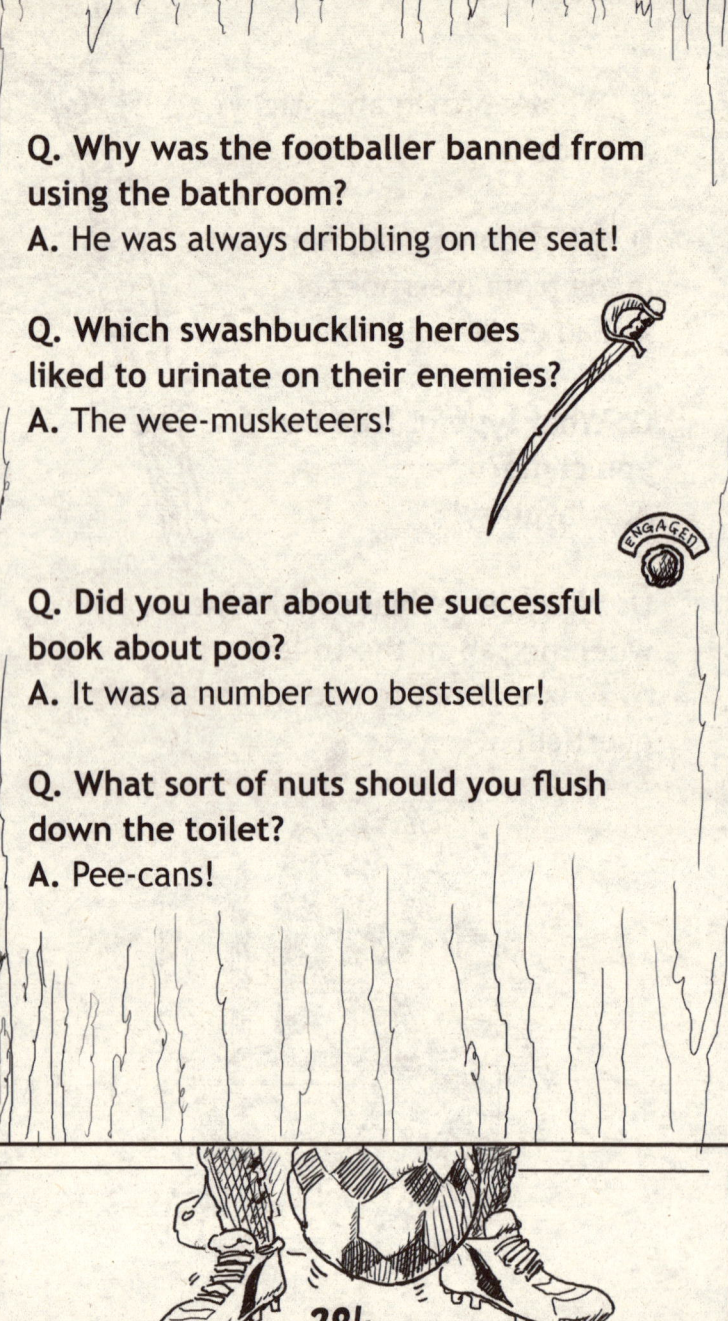

Q. Did you hear about the successful book about poo?
A. It was a number two bestseller!

Q. What sort of nuts should you flush down the toilet?
A. Pee-cans!

Q. What happened to the plumber who found a million pounds in the sewer?
A. He got stinking rich!

Q. Did you hear the gossip about the giant with diarrhoea?
A. It's all over town!

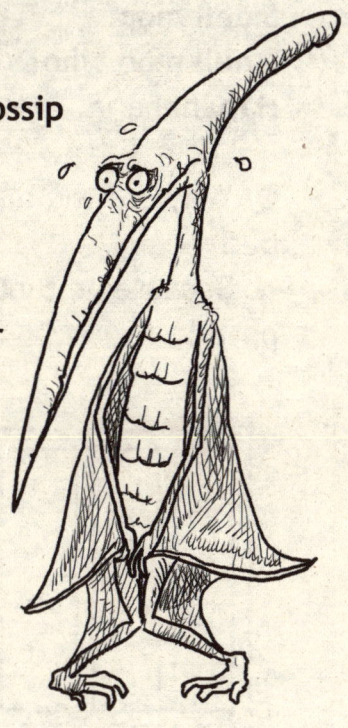

Q. Why can't you hear a pterodactyl going to the toilet?
A. Because the 'p' is silent!

Q. What's the difference between roast beef and pea soup?
A. Anyone can roast beef...

Q. Did you hear about the constipated maths teacher?
A. He worked it out with a pencil!

Knock, knock.
Who's there?
Smell mop.
Smell mop who?
Hahahahaha.

Q. Why did the madman hide under the bed?
A. Because he thought he was a little potty!

Windy Wisecracks

Q. What is the sharpest thing in the world?
A. A fart. It goes through your pants and doesn't even leave a hole!

Q. What is it called when the Royal family farts?
A. Noble gas!

Q. What does the Queen do after she burps?
A. Issues a royal pardon!

Q. Which king used to break wind at the dinner table?
A. Richard the Lionfart!

Q. Which queen always burped at the dinner table?
A. Queen Hic-toria!

Q. What has a bottom at the top?
A. Your legs!

Q. What do you call a very windy dinosaur?
A. A Stinkosaurus!